MRP II:
Making It
Happen

MRP II: Making It Happen

The Implementers' Guide to Success with Manufacturing Resource Planning

Thomas F. Wallace
Foreword by Walter E. Goddard

THE *Oliver Wight* COMPANIES®

The Oliver Wight Companies
Essex Junction, VT 05452

ISBN: 0-939246-04-X

Printed in the United States of America by Maple-Vail Book Manufacturing Company.

10 9 8 7 6 5 4 3

This book is dedicated, with
deep gratitude and an enduring
sense of loss, to

Ollie Wight

who led the way.

Contents

Foreword

Avoid being a pioneer! That's good advice for executives of manufacturing companies. Those who go first have the painful "arrows of surprises" sticking out. Undertaking a major change is a tough enough challenge without having to be the trailblazer. A trailblazer must find the path and chart the course. Those who follow will improve it and eventually make it a routine journey.

Competition guarantees that a manufacturing executive cannot avoid challenges. What he or she can often do, however, is avoid surprises. Surprises, even the good ones, mean that you have lost control. This book addresses these issues—it describes a controlled approach to helping your company become more competitive.

Manufacturing Resource Planning, MRP II, has proven to be an effective management weapon. It has enabled a great many companies to manage their business more professionally. With the excellent planning and scheduling information it provides, the successful MRP II users have made dramatic increases in customer service, significant gains in productivity, much higher inventory turns, and large reductions in purchase costs.

The two key terms that occur throughout this book are Class A MRP II and the *Proven Path*. Class A MRP II represents the destination and the *Proven Path* describes how to get there. Although Class A is not the ultimate (those that reach it continue to improve), it is a tough, attainable, and high payback target. Although the *Proven Path* may not be the only way to attain Class A, it is the most traveled one.

For you, this is a book of foresight. It lays out a direction, identifies activities, describes significant milestones, and leads you to a specific destination. By following the steps, you take advantage of the hundreds of companies that have preceded you. Thus, it really is a book of hindsight. It reflects what has been learned, both the prerequisites to be successful as well as the pitfalls to be avoided.

When looking backwards, three trailblazing events stand out, deserving special mention.

In 1976, Oliver Wight asked Darryl Landvater, President of Oliver Wight Video Productions, Inc., to analyze how certain companies had implemented MRP II so successfully. The result was a time-phased chart called the Implementation Plan, displaying the critical activities and the sequence in which they should occur. Although it has seen some modifications over the years, a testimonial to Darryl's good work is that it largely resembles the original presentation. The current chart is referenced throughout this book.

The second event was the creation of the ABCD Checklist by Ollie Wight in 1977. Ollie created this measurement system to focus people's attention on the operating aspects of MRP II rather than simply the technical, computer, and software aspects. More importantly, Ollie wanted to inspire users to operate it to its full potential. Installing an MRP II system means no more than having an opportunity to help your company. What counts is how well you are managing your business with an MRP II system.

In 1979, Oliver Wight Education Associates was formed to offer a complete curriculum of classes on MRP II. George Bevis and Tom Wallace teamed up to teach "MRP II: Successful Implementation." Tom had consulted with a wide variety of companies that had implemented MRP II systems and George, as Senior Vice President of the Tennant Company, had installed and operated one of the very best MRP II systems in our country. They put together a formal project plan containing the detailed steps required for the project team and the steering committee. This was the third important event in the evolution of this book.

Tom continues our tradition of helping practitioners. He has identified what it takes to become a Class A MRP II user and explains it clearly with real-world examples. Resist the "not invented here, let's do it our way" group. Blundering into MRP II, as too many companies do, will likely make your company better. Following the *Proven Path,* however, can make your company enormously better. Tom's advice is sound. His words and your actions can produce outstanding results for your company. We wish you a successful journey.

Walter E. Goddard
Sunapee, New Hampshire

Acknowledgments

I'm deeply grateful to a large number of people for their help in writing this book.

From within the Oliver Wight group, I'd like to say thanks a million to my Atlanta buddies Dave Garwood and John Civerolo; to Andre Martin, who routinely reinforces my affection for Canadians; to my partners in the Five-Day Class, John Dougherty and Bob Stahl; to two other good friends in New England, Chris Gray and Larry Wilson; to the West Coast contingent, which includes Roger Brooks, Jim Correll, Norris Edson, Al Stevens and Dave Waliszewski; to my fellow Midwesterners George Bevis, Lloyd Hager, Bill Jones, Ray Reed and John Schorr; to my fellow North Carolinians Dick Ling and John Sari; to John DeVito and Richard Norman, whom I'm still waiting to see on "Dallas"; and to Pete Skurla, who is living proof that New Jersey, contrary to the opinions of some, really is a class act.

The guys listed above helped enormously. There are, however, three people whose advice, encouragement and commitment of time was above and beyond. Walt Goddard not only wrote the Foreword to this book, but provided excellent input. Ollie Wight referred to Walter as his "severest and best critic." Once again, Ollie hit it right on the button. Bill Hartman was enormously helpful in bringing me down the learning curve for much of the material in Chapter 6. It wasn't easy, but Bill persevered. Darryl Landvater is owed special thanks on two counts, first of all, for his superb feedback and suggestions. Secondly, some years ago, Darryl authored the "Detailed MRP II Implementation Plan." This document, reproduced in Appendix C, represents the framework around which this entire book is structured. This book would not have been possible, at least at this time, without Darryl's earlier work as a foundation. Thank you, my friends.

Thanks to my editors, Bill Farragher and Deb Nelson, and to my publisher, Dana Scannell. Their superb assistance made this task far less difficult than it might have been. Thanks, also, to Jennifer Smith for her help with the production of this book.

Next, I send a tip of the hat and a deeply grateful "thank you" to the other members of the Wallace family: Evelyn, Dave, Anne, and M. C., for their support and understanding during the writing of this book. Along the way, they discovered they possessed reservoirs of patience hitherto unknown. With tongue in cheek, they refer to the entire process as a "character building experience." Thanks and God bless.

Most of all, I'm deeply indebted to the users, the people in manufacturing companies who've made it work. The early implementers in particular displayed great vision and courage to persevere, to take two steps forward and then maybe one step back, to keep the faith and to make it happen. Thanks largely to them, a trial and error approach to implementing MRP II is no longer necessary.

Thomas F. Wallace
Cincinnati, Ohio
and
Bryson City, North Carolina

How to Use This Book

A large part of the audience for this book falls into two categories:

- people from companies implementing MRP II, to use as a working guidebook.
- people from companies considering MRP II, who want to learn about what's involved in implementing it.

For people in companies implementing MRP II, the primary audiences are the executive steering committee and the MRP II project team. (Both of these groups are described in Chapter 5.) Ideally, all of these people would read the entire book, but that may not always be practical. Therefore, I recommend the following as a workable minimum:

- The "torchbearer" (the chairman of the executive steering committee, also described in Chapter 5): Read all chapters.
- Other members of the executive steering committee: Read Chapters 2, 4, 5, and 6 and the section of Chapter 9 which deals with implementing production planning.
- All full-time members of the MRP II project team: Read all chapters.
- Other members of the project team: Read Chapters 2 through 6, and 8 through 10.

People in the second category, from companies considering MRP II but not yet implementing, may want to read the entire book, and that's fine. However, if pressed for time, they should get most of what they need to know from Chapters 1 through 6.

Then, if a subsequent decision is made to implement MRP II, they can read the remaining chapters and perhaps revisit some of the material in the first six.

The Implementers' Checklists

This book is intended to be a working handbook for people involved in MRP II implementation. As such, it contains a series of Implementers' Checklists, to help guide the company down the implementation path. The first checklist appears at the end of Chapter 4, and there is one at the end of each remaining chapter. By using these checklists faithfully, a company can *ensure* a successful implementation of MRP II, and thus, the benefits that come from it.

MRP II:
Making It
Happen

Chapter 1

MRP II—Manufacturing Resource Planning

Manufacturing Resource Planning is helping to transform our industrial landscape. It's making possible profound improvements in the way manufacturing companies are being managed in North America, in Western Europe, and in Japan. A hundred years from now, when someone writes the definitive industrial history of the twentieth century, the evolution of MRP II will be viewed as a watershed event.

A detailed and precise definition of Manufacturing Resource Planning is contained in the Glossary in the back of this book (Appendix F). A less precise but perhaps more user-friendly definition of MRP II is:

a management system based on network scheduling.

Or another:

organized common sense.

Here are some others, perhaps not definitions but certainly darn good *descriptions*.

MRP II is a company increasing its sales by 20% in the face of an overall industry decline. Discussing how it happened, the vice president of sales explained:

"We're capturing lots of business from our competition. We can out-deliver 'em. Thanks to MRP II, we ship quick and we ship on time."

MRP II is a plant reducing its work week from one of heavy overtime down to a normal forty hours and simultaneously increasing output. The second shift general foreman:

"Our overtime reduction is due to the good schedules and future visibility that we get from MRP II. We're getting more throughput out of this plant in *five* days than we used to get in seven."

MRP II is a purchasing department reducing its purchase cost by 5%, in the face of heavy inflation. The director of purchasing:

"Thanks to MRP II, we're able to give our vendors consistently valid due dates—for the first time ever—and that makes it a lot easier for them to supply us. Further, our buyers are no longer in 'order launch and expedite' mode. They now have time to do the really important part of their job, which is to save money for the company."

MRP II is a company building an excellent Just-In-Time program on top of its already superb MRP II system. The production & inventory control manager:

"We were doing Just-In-Time before we ever heard that term. We're now turning our inventory over forty times per year; we're on our way to fifty; and I'm confident that we'll hit one hundred turns before long. There is no way we could be getting these kind of Just-In-Time results in this plant without MRP II."

That's MRP II. Here's how it came to be.

The Evolution of MRP II

MRP II began life in the 1960s as Material Requirements Planning. Its inventors were looking for a better method for ordering material and parts, and they found it in this technique. The logic of Material Requirements Planning asks the following questions:

- What are we going to make?
- What does it take to make it?
- What do we have?
- What do we have to get?

Ollie Wight called this the Universal Manufacturing Equation. He pointed out that its logic applies wherever things are being produced—whether they be jet aircraft, tin cans, machine tools, chemicals, cosmetics . . . or Thanksgiving dinner.

Material Requirements Planning simulates the Universal Manufacturing Equation. It uses the master production schedule (What are we going to make?), the bill of material (What does it take to make it?) and inventory records (What do we have?) to determine future requirements (What do we have to get?).

It quickly evolved, however, into something more than merely an ordering tool. Early users soon found Material Requirements Planning contained capabilities far greater than merely giving better signals for reordering. They learned this technique could help *keep* order due dates valid *after* the orders had been released to production or to vendors. It could detect when the *due date* of an order (when it's scheduled to arrive) was out of phase with its *need date* (when it's required).

This was a breakthrough. For the first time ever in manufacturing, there was a formal mechanism for keeping priorities valid in a changing manufacturing environment.

In manufacturing, conditions change constantly. Change is not simply a possibility, or even a probability. It's a certainty, the only constant, the only sure thing. The function of keeping order due dates valid and in synchronization with these changes is known as *priority planning,* or *scheduling.*

Did this breakthrough solve all of the problems? Was this all that was needed? Hardly. In manufacturing, the issue of priority is only half the battle. Another factor, capacity, represents an equally challenging problem. See Figure 1-1.

Techniques for helping plan capacity requirements were tied in with Material Requirements Planning. Tools were developed to

Figure 1-1

Priority	Capacity
Which ones?	Enough?
Sequence	Volume
Scheduling	Loading

support the planning of aggregate production levels (production planning), and the development of the specific build schedule (master production scheduling). Systems to aid in executing the plan were tied in: shop floor control for the "inside factory" and vendor scheduling for the "outside factory," the vendors. These developments resulted in the third step in this evolution: closed loop MRP. See Figure 1-2.

Closed loop MRP has a number of important characteristics:

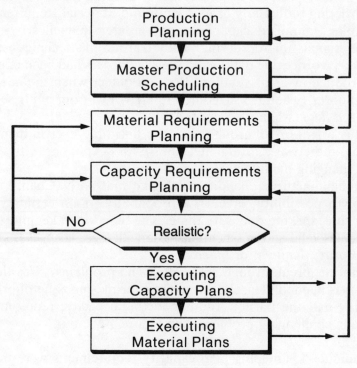

Figure 1-2

1. It's a *series of functions,* not merely Material Requirements Planning.

2. It contains tools to address both priority and capacity, and to support both planning and execution.

3. It has provisions for *feedback* from the execution functions back into the planning functions. This enables the plans to be altered when necessary, thereby keeping priorities valid as conditions change.

The fourth and most recent step in the evolution of MRP is called *Manufacturing Resource Planning,* or MRP II. It's a direct outgrowth and extension of closed loop MRP. Two additional elements are involved:

1. Finance—the ability to "translate" the operating plan (in pieces, pounds, gallons, each) into financial terms (dollars).

2. Simulation—the ability to ask "what if" questions and to obtain comprehensive, detailed, actionable answers—in both units and dollars.

This book deals with how to implement Manufacturing Resource Planning—all of the functions contained within closed loop MRP, plus finance and simulation.

Class ABCD

By the mid-1970s the term "MRP" had become a buzzword. Almost everyone, it seemed, was "doing MRP." Many companies were not happy with their results. On the other hand, some companies were achieving spectacular results from using it. Companies' reactions to MRP ranged from "It hasn't helped us at all" to "It's terrific; we couldn't run the business without it."

It became obvious that there were profound differences in how well companies were *using* this set of tools. To help focus on this issue, Ollie Wight developed the *ABCD* classification. See Figure 1-3.

Notice the second point under Class D—"another computer

Figure 1-3 Class ABCD[1]—Characteristics

Class A
• Uses the system to manage the business
• Works in all, or virtually all, areas of the business
• Outstanding results

Class B
• Uses the system to schedule and load
• Works primarily in manufacturing and materials
• Very good results

Class C
• Uses the system to order
• Works primarily in the production & inventory control department
• Fair to good results

Class D
• "Works" in data processing, but nowhere else
• Viewed as "another computer failure"
• Results: disappointment, frustration, wasted time and money

[1] See Appendix B for the ABCD Checklist, a self-evaluation tool by which companies can evaluate how well they're doing with MRP II, and where they need to improve.

failure." This strikes me as a bum rap for the computer, because the computer is the only element that's doing its job.

Has the computer failed? No, it's working. Has MRP II failed? Not really; it hasn't had a chance. What has failed? The *people* in the company. They've failed to implement and operate the system successfully.

This book deals with how to implement Manufacturing Resource Planning at a Class A level.

The Applicability of MRP II

Manufacturing Resource Planning has been successfully implemented in the following environments:

- conventional manufacturing (fabrication and assembly)
- fabrication only (no assembly)
- assembly only (no fabrication)
- repetitive manufacturing
- process manufacturing
- high-speed manufacturing
- low-speed manufacturing
- make-to-stock
- make-to-order
- engineer-to-order
- complex product
- simple product
- job shop
- flow shop
- manufacturers with distribution networks

Manufacturing Resource Planning has virtually unlimited application potential.
This book deals with how to implement Class A MRP II in any of the above environments.

MRP II as a Foundation

Today, there is a wide variety of tools and techniques that have been designed to help companies and their people produce their products better. These include Robotics, Just-In-Time, Quality Circles, CAD/CAM, Group Technology, Statistical Process Control and more. These are excellent tools. They have enormous potential.

But . . . none of them will ever yield their full potential unless they're coupled to *an effective planning and scheduling system.* Here's why:

It does little good to be extremely efficient . . . at producing the wrong items.

It does little good to make items at a very high level of quality . . . if they're not the ones needed.

It does little good to work hard at reducing set-up times and cutting lot sizes . . . if bad schedules prevent knowing what's really needed and when.

Manufacturing Resource Planning, when operating at a Class A level, will do several things for a company. Of and by itself, it will generate enormous benefits. Many companies have experienced, as a direct result of MRP II, dramatic increases in on-time shipments and productivity with simultaneous substantial decreases in lead times, purchase costs, quality problems and inventories.

Further, MRP II can provide the foundation upon which additional productivity and quality enhancements can be built . . . an environment where these other tools and techniques can reach their full potential.

One of my colleagues, Bob Stahl, has an excellent way of focusing on MRP II's role. Here, Bob says, is the *wrong* way to view it:

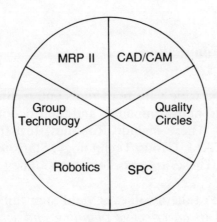

Figure 1-4

"Which one should we do first?" says an understandably confused CEO.

Here's how it looks when viewed properly:

J U S T I N T I M E	C A D / C A M	Statistical Process Control	Group Technology	R O B O T I C S	Quality Circles

VALID SCHEDULES
(MRP II)

Figure 1-5

Scheduling—knowing routinely what is needed and when via the formal system—is fundamental to productivity. MRP II is the vehicle to get valid plans and schedules, not only of materials and parts and production. It also means valid schedules of shipments to customers, of manpower and machine requirements, of required engineering resources, of cash flow and profit. MRP/MRP II is the foundation, the bedrock, for true productivity.

The meaning is clear: To get the most results the fastest, first implement MRP II at a Class A level. This issue will be discussed again in Chapter 11, which deals with operating MRP II after it's been implemented successfully.

Chapter 2

The Implementation Challenge

Catch-22

There's a "Catch 22" involved in implementing MRP II success-fully. It goes like this:

It's a whole lot of work. Implementing MRP II properly requires a great deal of time and effort on the parts of many people throughout the company. Many things must be done: data must be made more accurate, much education must take place, new software must be acquired and installed, new policies and procedures must be developed and made operational, and on and on.

It's a do-it-yourself project. Successful implementations are done internally. Virtually all of the work involved must be done by the company's own people. The responsibility can't be turned over to outsiders such as consultants or software vendors. That's been tried repeatedly, and hasn't been shown to work well at all. Where implementation responsibility is decoupled from operational responsibility, who can legitimately be accountable for results? If results aren't forthcoming, the implementers can claim the users aren't operating it properly, while the users can say that it wasn't implemented correctly. Almost without exception, the companies who have become Class A have been the ones where the users themselves implemented MRP II.

It's not the number one priority in the company. The first priority is to make shipments, meet the payroll, keep the equipment running . . . to run the business. All other activities must be subordinate. Implementing MRP II can't be number one, but it does need to be pegged as a very high number two priority.

This Catch-22 is one of the reasons why many companies that implement MRP II never get beyond Class C. Other reasons include:

It's people-intensive. MRP II is commonly misperceived as a computer system. Not so. It's a *people* system made possible by the computer.

Many early attempts at implementation focused on the computer and the software. They neglected the people. Ollie Wight said it well: "If you consider MRP II as a computer system to order parts, what you'll probably wind up with is a computer system to order parts. On the other hand, if you look upon MRP II as a set of tools with which to run the business far more effectively, and if you implement it correctly, that's exactly what you'll get."

Well, who runs the business? People do. People like foremen, engineers, marketeers, buyers, planners—and their managers—and their managers' managers, up to and including the general manager.[1]

It involves virtually every department within the company. It's not enough for just manufacturing, or materials, or distribution to be "on board." Virtually all departments in the company must be deeply involved in implementing MRP II; those mentioned plus marketing, engineering, quality, finance, personnel, etc.

It requires people to do their jobs differently. Most companies implementing MRP II must undergo massive behavior change

[1] Throughout this book, I'll use the term general manager to refer to the senior executive in charge of the business unit (company, division, plant) implementing MRP II. In this context, general manager can be synonymous with president, chief executive officer, chief operating officer, managing director, division manager, and in certain larger operations, plant manager.

to be successful. MRP II requires a "new set of values." Many things must be done differently, and this kind of transformation is never easy to achieve.

Experienced users say implementing MRP II is far more difficult than building a new plant, introducing a new product, or entering a whole new market. Breaking through the Catch-22, overcoming the people problems, making it happen—these are the challenges.

That's the bad news.

The good news is there's a way to meet these challenges. There's no mystery involved. Implementing MRP II successfully can be almost a sure thing—*if it's done right*. Yes, it is a lot of work. But it's virtually no risk—*if you do it right*. MRP II has never failed to work, not once, when correctly implemented. It *will* work and users will realize enormous benefits.

"Doing it right" involves two major elements:

1. An aggressive implementation schedule, supported by a massive mobilization of the company's resources.

2. The *Proven Path*. A set of eleven steps to take to ensure a successful implementation.

An Aggressive Implementation Schedule

The question arises: "How long should it take to implement all of MRP II, from when we start until we reach Class A?" First of all, it's very difficult to do in less than a year. Very few companies have ever achieved Class A status in less than twelve months. Why? Simply because so many things need to be done: massive education, data integrity, changing the way the business is run. And all the while, it's not the number one priority.

On the other hand, if it's taking a company (division, plant, unit) longer than two years, they're probably not doing it right. As a matter of fact, if a company takes longer than two years to implement, the odds for succeeding decrease sharply. It becomes more and more difficult to maintain the intensity, the enthusiasm, the drive and dedication necessary—and to keep MRP II pegged as a high number two priority.

Therefore, plan on it taking longer than one year, and less than two. For purposes of simplicity and consistency, let's pick the mid-point and routinely refer to an eighteen-month implementation.

Some people feel an eighteen-month time frame is too aggressive—too ambitious. It's not. It's a very practical matter, and it's also necessary. Here's why:

- *Intensity and enthusiasm.* MRP II will be implemented by users, the people running the business. Their first priority *must* be running the business, a full-time job in itself. Now, their responsibilities for implementing MRP II will require more work and more hours . . . above and beyond running the business.

  With a long, extended project, these people become discouraged. The payoff is too far in the future. There's no light at the end of the tunnel.

  However, with an aggressive schedule, these people can see progress being made early on. They can expect that things will start to improve substantially within a year or so. In our experience, the operating people—foremen, buyers, sales and marketing people, engineers, planners, etc.—respond favorably to this environment.

- *Priority.* The MRP II project must be given a very high priority, right behind running the business and making shipments. However, it's quite unlikely MRP II can hold such a high priority over three or four years. (Companies are like people; their attention spans are limited.) As the project's priority drops, so do the odds for success.

  The best approach is to establish MRP II as a very high priority; implement it quickly and successfully. And then capitalize on it. Build on it. Use it to help run the business better and better.

- *Change.* Change comes in two forms: changes in people, and changes in operating environment. Each type represents a threat to the MRP II project.

  Regarding people changes, take the case of a division whose general manager is MRP II-knowledgeable, enthusiastic and leading the implementation effort. Suppose this person is suddenly promoted to the corporate office. The new general manager is an unknown quantity. That person's reaction to MRP II will have a major impact on the project's chances for success. He[2] may oppose MRP II for some reason and the entire implementation effort will be at risk.

  Environmental change includes factors such as a sharp increase in business ("we're too busy to work on MRP II"), a sharp decrease in business ("we can't afford MRP II"), competitive pressures, new governmental regulations, etc.

  While such changes can certainly occur during an eighteen-month project, they're twice as likely to occur in a three-year project.

- *Schedule slippage.* In a major project like implementing MRP II, it's easy for schedules to slip. Throughout this book, I'll discuss ways to minimize slippage. For now, let me just point out an interesting phenomenon: in many cases, tight aggressive schedules are actually *less* likely to slip than loose, casual, non-aggressive schedules.

- *Benefits.* Taking longer than necessary to implement defers getting the benefits. The lost opportunity cost of only a *one month* delay can, for many companies, exceed a hundred thousand dollars. A *one year* delay could easily range into the millions.

---

[2] People who work in companies can be classified into two general categories: male and female. Any job category referenced in this book—be it general manager, vice president, department head, sales person, foreman, buyer, planner or direct labor person—in this writer's opinion can be very successfully performed by females. For purposes of simplicity and ease of reading, "he," "him," and "his" will be used throughout the book to refer to a person, be it male or female. Therefore, if it pleases the reader, "he," "him," and "his" can be read as "he or she" and "his or her."

An aggressive implementation schedule, therefore, is very desirable. But . . . is it practical? Yes, almost always. To understand how, we need to understand the concept of the "three knobs."

The Three Knobs

In project management, there are three primary variables: the amount of *work* to be done; the amount of *time* available (calendar time, not "man-years"); and the amount of *resources* available to accomplish the work. Think of these as three knobs, which can be adjusted.

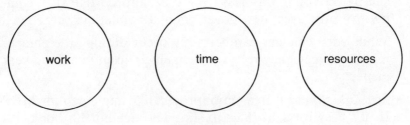

Figure 2-1

It's possible to hold any two of these knobs constant by varying the third. The workload is a constant, a given. The time should also be considered a constant, and is fixed at about eighteen months. Therefore, management can adjust the resource "knob," usually by increasing it. This is the right way to do it.

The wrong approach is to accept resources as fixed and constant. Then either the time knob must be increased, resulting in a longer project, or the work knob is decreased, increasing the risk of an unsuccessful project. Developing a proper cost justification can put the resource issue into clearer focus, and I'll return to this issue later. (See Chapter 4.)

Some people ask about the existing Class A companies. Did they all do it in eighteen months? Certainly not. Many of them took much longer, because they implemented in the late 1960s and 1970s. In those days, there just wasn't the body of knowledge about how to implement that's available now. In the early and mid-1980s, more and more companies have achieved Class A in less than two years. I think there's a form of learning curve here. As the number of successful implementations doubles, it takes "X" percent less time to implement.

The Proven Path

There's no longer any mystery how to do it. There exists a clearly defined set of steps that will guarantee a successful Class A implementation in a short time frame if followed faithfully. Those steps are called the *"Proven Path."*

There's a tested, proven way to implement. A dozen or so years ago, no one could say that. Back then, people said—

"It should work."

"We really believe it'll work."

"It stands a good chance of working."

"It certainly ought to work."

No more. There's no longer any doubt. *If you do it right, it will work.* Period. And you can take that to the bank.

How can we be so certain? How did this become such a thing? What happened along the way from then till now?

The main reason centers on some executives and managers in certain North American manufacturing companies. They had several things in common: a dissatisfaction with the status quo, a belief that better tools to manage their business could be developed, and an ample supply of courage. These were the early implementers. They led the way.

Naturally, they had some help. Consultants and educators—people like my colleagues and I—assisted. Computer companies, most notably IBM in the early days, helped by developing generalized software packages for MRP, capacity planning, and shop floor control. But, fundamentally, the users did it themselves.

Over the past twenty years, thousands of companies have implemented MRP/MRP II. Some have implemented very successfully (Class A or B), many less so (Class C or D). By observing a great variety of these implementation attempts and their results, it's become very clear what works and what doesn't. The methods proven unworkable have been discarded. The things that work have been refined, developed, and synthesized into what we call the *Proven Path*.

The *Proven Path* isn't theory; it's not blue sky or something dreamed up over a long weekend in Colorado Springs, where the air's real thin. Rather, it's a product of the school of hard knocks, built out of scar tissue, trial and error, learning, testing, refining.

Surprising? Not really. The *Proven Path* evolved the same way MRP II did—pragmatic, practical, straightforward. It wasn't created in an ivory tower or a laboratory, but on the floors of our factories, in our purchasing departments, in our sales and marketing departments, and on our shipping docks.

The *Proven Path* consists of eleven steps. We'll take a very brief look at each one of these steps now, and discuss them more thoroughly in subsequent chapters. They are:

1. *First-Cut Education.* A handful of executives and operating managers from within the company must learn about MRP II before they can do a proper job of step number two (Cost Justification and Commitment).

2. *Cost Justification and Commitment.* The principle here is, "Don't buy a pig in a poke." After these key executives and managers have learned about MRP II in First-Cut Education, they should put pencil to paper and calculate the expected costs and benefits.[3] If the benefits, both tangible and intangible, don't justify the costs, the company should stop there, and not spend any more money on MRP II. If the numbers are compelling and

---

[3] Some benefits may be largely intangible, and therefore, very difficult to quantify. Where these intangible benefits are seen to be very important, they should be identified in the cost justification, even though they may not be quantified.

all of the key people believe them, then they can make a commitment to doing it right.

3. *User-Controlled Project Team.* To succeed, each element of MRP II must be implemented by the same people who will be held accountable for operating it after it goes on the air. The project team is made up primarily of users, and is responsible for implementing MRP II at the *operational* level in the company.

4. *Full-Time Project Leader.* At least one key person from within the company should be freed from all other responsibilities to manage the implementation effort. There needs to be at least one person within the company for whom MRP II is priority number one. A part-time project leader will very often have to give preference to operational responsibilities at the expense of working on MRP II. This will cause the project to slow down and will decrease the odds for success.

5. *Executive Steering Committee.* To ensure success, top management must provide high level leadership and must carry overall accountability for results. "The buck stops here." The steering committee is the means by which the general manager and his staff lead the entire implementation process. Without frequent top management reviews of progress, the project will tend to drift, and the odds for success will drop.

6. *Professional Guidance.* MRP II is not an extension of past experience. It's a whole new way of running a company. Companies implementing MRP II need periodic access to someone who has "been there"—someone who has been deeply involved in one or more Class A implementations—to serve as a catalyst, a sounding board, a giver of advice and, most important, as a "conscience" to top management.

7. *Education of the Critical Mass.* A minimum of 80% of *all* of the people in the company need to receive education on MRP II prior to implementation, with the balance shortly thereafter. For MRP II to succeed, many things will have to change, including the way that many people do their jobs. People need to know what, why, and how these changes will affect them. People need to be led to see the need to do their jobs differently, and the benefits that will result.

8. *Pilot Approach to MPS/MRP.* Don't play "you bet your company." Prove that master production scheduling and material requirements planning are working satisfactorily on a pilot group, before cutting over all products and parts.

9. *Close the Loop.* Tie in the execution systems—shop floor control, vendor scheduling, etc.—into the planning systems.

10. *Finance and Simulation.* Integrate the operational systems with the financial systems. Begin to use the "what-if" capability.

11. *Dedication to Continuing Improvement.* Once a company reaches Class A, it has to keep working hard at making it better and better. It can then begin to use its Class A system as the "launch pad" for further progress.

The *Proven Path* is a logical, straightforward implementation approach, based completely on demonstrated results. As I said earlier, it is a lot of work but virtually no risk. If a company follows the *Proven Path* faithfully, sincerely and vigorously, it will become Class A—and within two years.

Chapter 3

Implementation Strategy

Strategy

"It's possible to swallow an elephant . . . one chunk at a time."

"Be aggressive. Make deliberate haste. Implement in eighteen months or less."

Those two concepts may sound contradictory, but they're not. There's a way to "swallow the elephant a chunk at a time" and still get there quickly. Here's the strategy:

1. Divide the total MRP II implementation project into three major phases, to be done *serially*—one after another.

2. Within each phase, accomplish a variety of individual tasks *simultaneously*.

For most companies, implementing all of MRP II is simply too much to handle at one time. The sum of the "chunks" is simply too much to digest all at once. That's the reason for the three-phase approach.

The simultaneous tasks within each phase are based on the need for an aggressive, eighteen-month implementation cycle. Doing each of the many tasks involved serially would simply take too long.

Let's examine what's to be done in each of the three phases:

Phase I—Basic MRP: Production Planning, Master Production Scheduling, Material Requirements Planning along with the support functions of Forecasting, Customer Order Entry, Inventory Accuracy, Bill of Material Accuracy and Structure, plus Anticipated Delay Reporting from the shop floor and purchasing. Also, Distribution Resource Planning should be included here for companies with branch warehouses.

Basic MRP is not a stand-alone system. Of and by itself, it will produce only marginal results. It's merely the first major segment; it builds the foundation for the subsequent phases.

Phase II—Closing The Loop: Shop Floor Control, Capacity Requirements Planning and Input/Output Control for the factory, supported by routing accuracy; Vendor Scheduling for the "outside factories," i.e., the vendors.

Phase III—Finance and Simulation: Tying the financial systems into the MRP II operational data base, and activating the "what-if" capability of MRP II. Other elements may also be included in Phase III that were identified earlier as very desirable but not absolutely necessary to achieve MRP II . . . e.g., automated shop data collection, an improved forecasting system, etc.

The chart in the back of the book is a graphic representation of the three-phase approach. This chart, and the text contained in Appendix C, represent the Detailed MRP II Implementation Plan developed by Darryl Landvater, a leading educator and consultant in the field.

Take a moment to study this bar chart. The three major phases, as well as the simultaneous activities within each phase, are outlined. In this generalized diagram, basic MRP begins at Time Zero and continues through Month 12; closed loop MRP through Month 15; and MRP II (financial planning and simulation) through Month 18.

Please be aware that this bar chart is generalized. It will not fit exactly into each and every company's situation. Examples:

• Some companies already have accurate and properly structured bills of material. They need to spend less time on this function than the chart indicates.

• Some companies don't have routings and standards. They have to start on them far earlier than what's shown.

• Some companies already have shop floor control. This means that the loop can be closed in manufacturing simultaneously with basic MRP.

On occasion, people question the location of Time Zero—the day the "clock starts ticking." Should it be at the very beginning of First-Cut Education, as shown by the yellow bar on the chart? Or should it be near the end of the red bar for the Justification and Commitment process? Quite frankly, there's no single answer to this question.

Some companies move through these first two steps quickly, so for them, the precise location of Time Zero is not terribly important. Other companies, however, find they need more time for these early activities than the two months implied by the length of their bars on the chart. In these cases, Time Zero would be *after* Justification and Commitment. The principles to be considered are:

1. Take as much time as needed to learn about MRP II, and build a consensus among the management team. Do the cost/benefit analysis. Make sure this is the direction the company wants to go. Then commit to the project.

2. Once the decision is made to go for it, pursue it aggressively.

Occasionally people have questions on the functional content of each of the three phases, such as "Why isn't shop floor control in Phase I? Can we move MRP to Phase II and production planning to Phase III?"

The timing of the implementation plan is structured to get the basic planning tools in place early. Companies that implement shop floor control before material requirements planning may get better time and attendance data and a better handle on job location, but probably not much more. The biggest benefit from shop floor control comes from its ability to prioritize the jobs on the shop floor effectively. It simply can't do that without valid order due dates, which is done through material requirements planning with feedback from the shop floor and purchasing. Feedback is essential even in Phase I. As basic MRP is implemented, the plant and purchasing must be geared up to notify the planning people of jobs which won't be complete on time. See Chapter 9 for details.

Material requirements planning can't do its job without a valid master production schedule, which must be in balance with the production plan. That's why these functions are in Phase I, and the execution functions (plus capacity requirements planning) are in Phase II.

Schedule by Function, Not Software Modules

Business functions and software modules are not the same things. A business function is just that: something that needs to be done to run the business effectively. Examples include planning for future capacity needs; maintaining accurate inventory records, bills of material, and routings; customer order entry and delivery promising, and so on.

Software modules are pieces of computer software which exist to support people in the effective execution of business functions.

Once in a while, I see companies involved in an MRP II implementation effort scheduling their project around tasks like: "Implement the SOE (Sales Order Entry) module," "Implement the ITP (Inventory Transaction Processing) module," "Implement the PDC (Product Data Control) module," etc. This is a misguided approach for two reasons: sequence and message.

Companies that build their project plan around implementing software modules often do so based on their software vendor's recommendation. This sequence may or may not be the best one to follow. In some cases, it merely slows down the project, which is serious enough. In others, it can greatly reduce the odds for success. One such plan recommended that the company install first the material requirements planning module, then the shop floor control module, then the master production scheduling module. Well, that's backwards. MRP can't work properly without the master schedule, and shop floor control can't work properly without MRP working properly. Following such a plan would have not only slowed down the project, but also would have substantially decreased the odds for success.

The second problem concerns the message that's sent out when the implementation effort is focused on software modules. Concentrating on "implementing software modules" sends exactly the wrong message. The primary emphasis is on the wrong thing— the computer. MRP II is *not* a computer system; it's a *people* system made possible by the computer. Implementing it is not a computer project or a systems project; it's a *management* project. The people in the company are changing the way they manage the business, so that they can manage it better than they ever could before.

People talk about the *ABCs* of implementing Manufacturing Resource Planning. The concept is derived from the old ABC approach to inventory control. In that technique, the A items are considered very significant, costly, important, etc. and, hence, deserve the most attention, the most careful planning. The B items are of less significance than the A items and, hence, less time is devoted to each one of them. The C items, while essential, are of least overall significance and are given proportionate attention.

This ABC approach, applied to implementation, identifies the computer as the C item, the hardware and software. It's essential; MRP II can't be done manually. But it's of lesser significance overall than the other elements.

The B item is the data: the inventory records, the bills of material, the routings, etc. They are more significant and require more of the company's overall attention and managerial emphasis.

The A item is the people. It's the key element in making it work, the most significant of all. If the people part of the implementation process is managed properly, then the people will understand the objectives and how to get there. They'll take care of getting the data accurate and keeping it accurate. They'll not allow the "computer tail" to wag the "computer dog," as has been the case far too often. The people are the key.

Special Situations

Those of us within the Oliver Wight organization repeatedly point out MRP II is a generalized set of tools that apply to *any* manufacturing company, as well as to many non-manufacturers.

We go to great lengths to help people break through the "we're unique" syndrome. When people recognize there is a well-defined, universally applicable body of knowledge in this field, they'll be able to use it to solve fundamental problems.

On the other hand, MRP II is a set of tools that must be tailored to fit individual companies. The implementation project must also reflect the individual company, its environment, its people, its processes, its history, etc. Here are some examples of special situations that can affect the specifics of implementation.

Process and Repetitive. These are companies with manufacturing methods that can be described as purely "process" (chemicals, food, plastics, etc.) or as highly "repetitive" (tin cans, automobiles, razor blades, etc.).

The overall concept of MRP II definitely applies in these kinds of manufacturing environments. However, each and every function within MRP II may not be necessary. One good example is shop floor dispatching on an operation-by-operation basis, which is typically needed only where there is a functional, "job shop" form of organization. Capacity requirements planning is another. In some process or repetitive plants, all of the necessary capacity planning can be done at the rough-cut level.

A company in this situation, not needing detailed shop dispatching and CRP, could exclude them from its implementation plan. And that's good news. It'll be easier to get to Class A— and quicker.

Re-implementers. Some companies have already attempted to implement MRP/MRP II, but it's not working properly. They have some or all of the technical pieces in place, yet they're not getting the results they should. Now they need to *re-implement,* but this time doing it right. Darryl Landvater said it well: "The jobs involved in improving an MRP II system are the same as those in implementing it correctly." The difference is that, for the re-implementer, some of the jobs may have already been done. For example, a re-implementer company may have already acquired a complete, or virtually complete, set of software for MRP II a few years before. Many of the software steps necessary for the first-time implementer wouldn't be required in this case.

Multi-plant. How about a company or division with more than one plant? How should they approach implementation?

Broadly, there are three choices: serial, simultaneous, or staggered.

Take the case of a company with four plants. Each employs hundreds of people, and has a reasonably complete support staff. The company wants to implement MRP II in all of its plants.

The *serial* approach to implementation calls for implementing completely in a given plant, then starting in the second plant and implementing completely there, etc. The schedule would look like Figure 3-1:

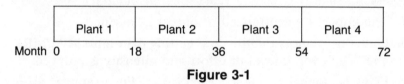

Figure 3-1

This time span is not acceptable. Seventy-two months is six years, and that's simply too long.

The *simultaneous* approach is to do them all at the same time, as in Figure 3-2.

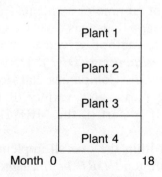

Figure 3-2

This approach looks good because the entire project is finished in eighteen months. However, there may be some problems with it. One of them would be availability of centralized resources, such as data processing, overall project management, etc. It may be impractical to support all four plants simultaneously.

Another potential problem gets back to the Catch-22 of MRP II. Implementing MRP II is not the first priority. Some companies may wisely conclude that implementing simultaneously in all plants could be more than they want to bite off at one time. The effort and intensity required may well have a negative effect on how well they're able to run the business.

This leads most companies to choose the *staggered* method shown in Figure 3-3.

This approach has several advantages:

1. It gets the whole company implemented fairly quickly (in this case, in slightly over two years for four plants).

2. The impact on centralized resources is lessened.

3. Only one plant is piloting and cutting over onto MPS/MRP at a time. The overall level of effort and intensity is reduced.

4. Plant personnel can teach each other. For example, users from Plant 2 may participate in the pilot and cutover at Plant 1. In so doing, they can learn from the first plant's mistakes and avoid them. Plant 3 people can learn and help at Plant 2, and so on.

One company brought all nine of its plants from Time Zero to Class A within three years. This was a very complex implementation, and the staggered method served them very well.

Distribution Resource Planning (DRP). DRP is MRP II for a network of field warehouses. Companies that stock finished products, or perhaps spare parts, at a variety of remote locations should implement DRP as part of the MRP II implementation project.

Where should it fit within the overall implementation? As indicated earlier, I recommend *DRP be implemented at the same time as basic MRP.* Here's why:

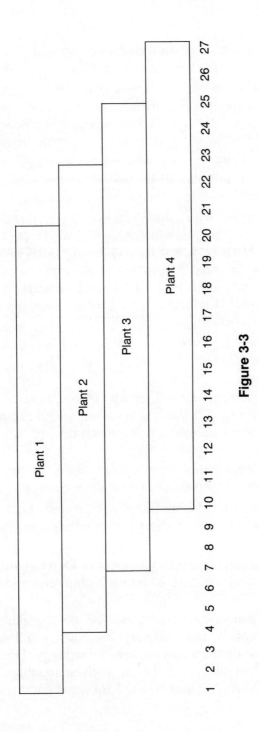

Figure 3-3

1. The functions involved are virtually identical: education, inventory accuracy, "bill of material" accuracy, item analysis, etc.

2. Different people are involved. For example, getting inventory accuracy at the branch warehouses should not affect the workload of the people getting inventory accuracy in the stockroom at the plant.

3. DRP can and should be piloted at the same time as the master scheduling/material requirements planning pilot.

4. In a company with a distribution network, master scheduling and material requirements planning will never work at full efficiency until DRP is operating. (Delaying DRP is analogous to implementing material requirements planning for some, but not all, levels in the bill of material.) Therefore, delaying DRP until the rest of MRP II is implemented means many months of less-than-complete benefits.

5. Implementing DRP first, then MRP II, means many months of deferral of *all* of the benefits from MRP II.

Necessary non-standard functions. Here I'm referring to functions necessary to run the business, but which are peculiar to a given company or industry. Some examples are:

1. The pharmaceutical industry, among many others, requires lot traceability and lot number inventory control.

2. Companies producing fashion goods need high flexibility of product design and a very short cycle to design, procure, produce and ship.

3. Firms supplying the Department of Defense are required to adhere to special contract accounting requirements.

There are many other examples. The message here is obvious: look very closely at the company, its industry and marketplace, its position within them, and its overall strategy. Don't make the serious error of assuming that if a given function isn't in the software package, it's not needed for your company. The new software may need to be modified to support the function in question, ideally enabling it to be done even better. Perhaps the software will need modification merely to allow the function to be done as before. Or perhaps no software changes will be necessary.

It's important for companies to do their homework on these types of issues. They need to ask "What kinds of special things are we doing today that we'll continue to have to do in the future after MRP II is on the air? Are they essential? If so, will they be handled within MRP II, or not? If not, how will we do them?"

Part of getting a better set of tools to run the business is to make certain that all of the necessary tools are in place.

Time Wasters

Nowhere on the *Proven Path* does one see things like:

- Document the current system
  or
- Design the new system

That's because these things are *time wasters* when done as separate activities.

Yes, it is necessary to identify those elements of today's operations which need to be blended into MRP II. What's *not* necessary is to spend time doing a detailed documentation of the current system, which is going to be replaced.

Yes, it's necessary to ensure that the details of how MRP II will be operated in the company will support the company's goals, operating environment and necessary functions. What's *not* necessary is to spend time re-inventing the wheel. The system is already "designed"; it's called MRP II. The issue is how, specifically and in detail, will the tools of MRP II be used to run the business.

The *Proven Path* approach makes provisions for these things to occur, not as separate steps, but as part of an integrated, logical process of managing the implementation of MRP II. The details will come later, in Chapters 5, 6 and 8.

In the following chapter, we'll examine closely the first two blocks on the *Proven Path:* First-Cut Education and Justification and Commitment.

Chapter 4

Cost Justification & Commitment

Justifying the cost of an MRP II project is essential. Here are four reasons why:

1. *Number two priority*. The number two priority in a company implementing MRP II needs to be just that: implementing MRP II. (Priority #1: Run the business, remember?) It's really difficult to keep MRP II pegged as a very high second priority if the relevant costs and benefits haven't been established. If MRP II doesn't carry a very high priority, the chances for success decrease.

2. *A solid commitment*. Implementing MRP II means changing the way the business is run. Top management and operating management must be committed to making it happen. Without a solid projection of costs and benefits, the deep degree of dedication may not be attainable, and the chances for success will decrease sharply.

3. *One allocation of funds*. By identifying costs thoroughly and completely before implementation, the company has to process only one spending authorization. This avoids repeated "trips to the well" and their attendant delays during the life of the project.

4. *Benchmarks*. A quantified set of anticipated benefits can serve as benchmarks down the road. After implementation, actual savings can be compared to those projected in the cost justification. Is the company getting the benefits that were projected? If not, why not? The people can then find out what's wrong, fix it, and start getting the benefits they targeted.

The first two steps on the *Proven Path* are First-Cut Education, and Justification and Commitment. See Figure 4-1.

First-Cut Education

Key people need to learn about MRP II before they can do a proper job of estimating costs and benefits. They need to learn:

1. What is MRP II?

2. Is it for us? Does it make sense for our business?

3. What will it cost?

4. What will it save? What are the benefits we'll get if we do it the right way and get to Class A?

Some companies attempt to cost justify MRP II before they understand what it's all about. Almost invariably, they'll underestimate the costs involved in implementation. They'll feel, "MRP is a computer system to order parts. Therefore, most of the costs will be computer-related." As a result, the project will not be properly funded.

Further, these companies almost always underestimate the benefits. They think, "MRP is a computer system to order parts; therefore, most of the benefits will come from inventory reduction." It then becomes very difficult to peg implementation as the second-highest priority in the company.

The obvious moral of the story: First, learn about it; then, cost justify it.

Who needs First-Cut Education? The same people involved in Cost Justification and Commitment. For a "typical" company, they would be:

1. *Top management:* The general manager and the vice presidents of engineering, finance, manufacturing, and marketing.

2. *Operating management:* Production manager(s), production control manager, purchasing manager, sales (customer service) manager, engineering manager, data processing manager.

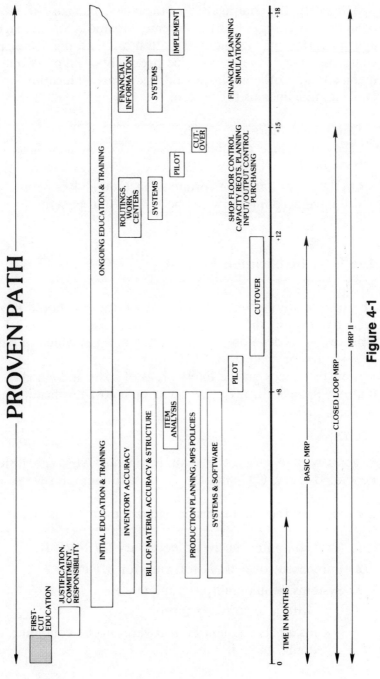

Figure 4-1

Obviously, the composition of this group can vary greatly from company to company. In smaller companies, top management and operating management are often one and the same. Larger companies may have senior vice presidents, directors, materials managers and others who would need early education on MRP II. The guidelines to follow are:

Don't send more people through First-Cut Education than necessary, since the final decision to implement hasn't yet been made.

On the other hand, be certain to include all key people who will have accountability for both costs and benefits.

The Cost Justification Process

The people who attended First-Cut Education should now proceed to develop the cost justification. (See Figure 4-2.) Their objective is to develop a set of numbers upon which to base the decision for or against MRP II.

Let's first focus on the likely areas of costs and benefits. After that, we'll work through several sample cost justifications.

COSTS

A good way to group the costs is via our ABC categories: A-People, B-Data, C-Computer. Let's take them in reverse order.

C-Computer. Include in this category the following costs:

1. New computer hardware necessary for MRP II.
2. Purchased (or leased) software for MRP II.
3. Systems people and programmers to:
   - write new software internally.
   - install the purchased software on the computer, debug it and make it work.

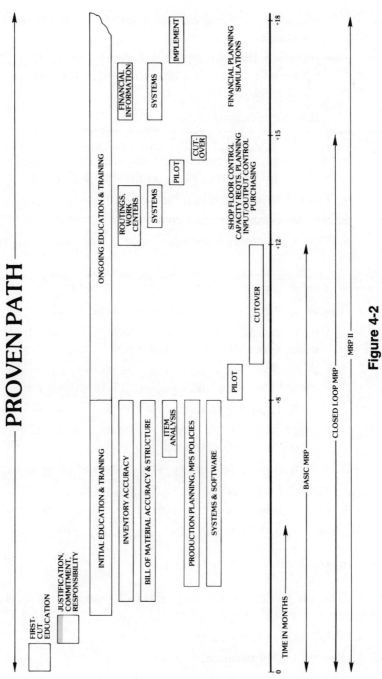

PROVEN PATH

Figure 4-2

- enhance the purchased software to make it functionally complete.
- interface the purchased software with existing systems which will remain in place after MRP II is implemented.
- assist in user training.
- develop documentation.
- provide system maintenance.

These people may already be on the staff, may have to be hired, and/or may be temporary "contract" personnel.

4. Forms, supplies, miscellaneous.

5. Software maintenance costs.

6. Other anticipated changes from the software vendor.

B-Data. Include here the costs involved to get and maintain:

1. Inventory record accuracy, which could involve:

- new fences, gates, scales, shelves, bins, lift trucks and other types of new equipment.
- costs associated with plant re-layout, sometimes necessary to create and/or consolidate stockrooms.
- cycle counting costs.
- other increases in manpower necessary to achieve and maintain inventory accuracy.

2. Bill of material accuracy, structure and completeness.

3. Routing accuracy.

4. Other elements of data such as forecasts, customer orders, item data, work center data, etc.

A-People. Include here costs for:

1. The project team, typically the full-time project leader and perhaps one or several assistants.

2. Education, including travel and lodging.

3. Professional guidance.

4. Increases in the indirect payroll, either temporary or on-going, not reflected elsewhere. Examples include perhaps a new master scheduler where there was none before, additional material planning people, another dispatcher, etc.

These are the major categories of cost for MRP II. In general terms, for an average-sized company, it'll cost around one million dollars. This number is not based on conjecture, but rather on the direct experience of many companies.

A survey, taken during the latter half of 1984, captured results from more than a thousand companies who had implemented MRP/MRP II.[1]

The average total cost of implementation, for all companies responding, was $907,000. As a part of the survey, companies were asked to rate themselves as Class A, B, C, or D. Interestingly, the Class A companies reported implementation costs of $1,181,000 while the companies who identified themselves as Class D reported average costs of $1,002,000. Interesting, eh? It has cost companies almost as much to be Class D as Class A.

BENEFITS

So much for the "bad news," i.e., the costs. Now let's look at the "good news," the areas of benefits.

1. *Increased sales,* as a direct result of improved customer service. MRP II enables many companies to:
- ship on time virtually all the time.
- ship in less time than the competition.
- have their salesmen spend their time selling, rather than expediting shipments and making excuses to customers over missed shipments.

In short, MRP II can come to represent a significant competitive weapon. The users' survey cited above showed customer service

---

[1] The results of this survey are published in the 1985 Newsletter of The Oliver Wight Companies, Newbury, New Hampshire.

gains of 16% for all respondents; 28% for the companies who identified themselves as Class A. For most companies, better customer service means more sales.

2. *Increased direct labor productivity,* resulting from the valid, attainable schedules which MRP II can enable companies to have. Productivity is increased via:

- providing matched sets of components to the assembly areas, thereby eliminating much of the inefficiency and idle time often present.
- reducing sharply the amount of expediting, lot splitting, emergency changeovers, short runs, etc., in the fabrication areas.
- requiring much less overtime, because the forward visibility provided by MRP II is so much better.

The survey results showed all respondents reporting an average productivity gain of 10%; the Class A users got 16%.

3. *Reduced purchase cost.* MRP II provides the tools to give vendors valid schedules and better forward visibility. Once the customer gets out of "order launch and expedite" mode, the vendors can produce the customer's items more efficiently, at lower cost. A portion of these savings can be passed back to the customer.

Further, valid schedules can free the buyers from a life of expediting and paper shuffling, so that they can do the really important parts of their jobs: sourcing, negotiation, contracting, value analysis, cost reduction, etc.

Survey results: All companies reported an average purchase cost reduction of 7%; the Class A companies got 11%. In many companies, the single largest financial benefit from MRP II comes from purchase cost reduction.

4. *Reduced Inventories.* Valid schedules mean matched sets of components, which means making the products on schedule and shipping them on time. That's the way to reduce the inventories.

In the survey, all companies reported an average inventory drop of 17%, and Class A companies saw 25%.

For most companies, the four benefit areas identified above are the big ones. However, there are other benefits from MRP II which are potentially very significant, and should not be overlooked. They include:

5. *Reduced obsolescence,* from an enhanced ability to manage engineering changes, better forward visibility, and a reduced overall risk of obsolescence due to lower inventories in general.

6. *Reduced quality costs.* Valid schedules can result in a more stable environment, which can mean less scrap. Eliminating the "end-of-the-month lump," where perhaps 75% of the shipments go out in the last 25% of the month, can mean reduced warranty costs.

7. *Reduced premium freight,* both inbound, by having a better handle on what's needed, and outbound, by being able to ship on time.

8. *Elimination of the annual physical inventory.* If the inventory numbers are accurate enough for MRP II, they'll be more than good enough for the balance sheet. Class A companies rarely take annual physical inventories. This can be a substantial savings in some companies, encompassing not only the costs of taking the inventory itself. Also involved are the costs of disrupting production, since many companies can't produce while they count.

9. *Increased productivity of the indirect workforce.* MRP II will help not only the direct labor people to be more productive, but also the indirect folks. An obvious example is the large expediting group maintained by some companies. Under MRP II this group should no longer be needed and its members could be absorbed into other, more productive jobs.

Another aspect of this, more subtle and perhaps difficult to quantify, is the increased productivity of the supervisors and managers. That includes foremen, engineers, quality control people, production managers, vice presidents of marketing, and let's not forget about the guy in the corner office: the general manager. They should all be able to do their jobs better when the company is operating with a valid game plan and an effective set of tools to help them execute it.

They'll have more fun, also. More satisfaction from a job well done. More of a feeling of accomplishment. That's called "quality of life." It's almost impossible to quantify that benefit, but it may be the most important one of all.

RESPONSIBILITY

The question is often asked: "Who should do the justification? Who should put the numbers together?"

Answer: no one single person. Rather, the participants in the justification process should be those executives and managers who'll be held accountable for achieving the projected benefits within the framework of the identified costs.

Here's an excellent way to do it:

1. A given department head, let's say the manager of sales administration and customer service, attends First-Cut Education.

2. Upon returning to the company, that person does some homework, focusing on what benefits the sales department would get from a Class A MRP II system, plus what costs might be involved.

3. The manager then schedules a meeting with his boss, let's say, the vice president of sales and marketing, who has also recently returned from First-Cut Education.

4. These people, working together, develop *their* numbers. In this example, the most likely benefit would be increased sales resulting from improved customer service, and the biggest cost elements might be in education and training.

Note the participative nature of this process. Top management as well as operating management is involved. This is far better than the more "traditional" approach, where the operating managers put together the cost justification and then attempt to "sell" the project to their bosses. If top management has been to First-

Cut Education, there should be no need for them to "be sold." Rather, they and their key managers should be "selling themselves" on specifically how MRP II will benefit their company, and what it'll cost to get to Class A.

Be fiscally conservative. When in doubt, estimate the costs to the high side of their probable range, and the benefits low. Don't promise more than you can deliver.

JUSTIFICATION EXAMPLES

To illustrate the process, let's create a hypothetical company, with the following characteristics:

Annual Sales: $80 Million

Employees: 750

Number of Plants: 1

Manufacturing Process: Fabrication and assembly

Product: A complex assembled product, make-to-order, with many options (electronics, machinery, etc.)

Pre-tax Net Profit: 8% of sales

Annual Direct Labor Cost: $8 Million

Annual Purchase Volume (production materials): $24 Million

Current Inventories: $18 Million

For convenience, we'll refer to this organization as Company T (for "Typical"). Let's take a look at their projected costs and benefits, but first a warning:

Beware! The numbers that follow are not your company's numbers. They are sample numbers only. Do not use them. They may be too high or too low for your specific situation. Using them could be hazardous to the health of your company and your career.

With that caution, let's examine the numbers. Costs are divided into "one-time" (acquisition) costs and "recurring" (annual operating) costs . . . and are in our three categories: C-Computer, B-Data, A-People. See Figure 4-3.

Figure 4-3 Company T Cost Justification

COSTS

C-Computer	One-time	Recurring	Comments
Hardware	$ 60,000	$36,000	Company T already has a computer, but will need to add some new hardware to it. Some of the new hardware will be purchased, and some leased at $3,000 per month.
Software	200,000	—	The most expensive software package being considered costs $200,000. They plan to maintain the software themselves, rather than buy the software vendor's maintenance service.
Systems and Programming	200,000	35,000	Data processing people costs to install the software, modify it to fit the business, interface it to existing systems, enhance it, maintain it, and to do documentation, training, etc.

B-Data	One-time	Recurring	Comments
Inventory Record Accuracy	235,000	30,000	Includes new equipment and one full-time cycle counter.
Bill of Material Accuracy and Structure	120,000	—	Bills will need to be restructured into the modular format. Experienced engineers will be required for this step.
Routing Accuracy	25,000	—	Routings are fairly accurate now, but will need to be reviewed.

A-People	One-time	Recurring	Comments
Project Team	$ 160,000	—	One full-time project leader and one assistant, for eighteen months.

A-People	One-time	Recurring	Comments
Outside Education	100,000	10,000	Includes travel.
Inside Education	80,000	20,000	Includes costs for video, overtime costs, plus vendor education.
Professional Guidance	25,000	2,000	One-day visits, every four to eight weeks, by an experienced MRP II professional.
Total Costs	$1,205,000	$133,000	

BENEFITS Function	Current	% Improvement	Annual Benefits	Comments
Sales	$80,000,000	5% at 8%	$320,000	Sales and marketing is projecting a 5% sales gain due to improved customer service. The company's net profit has been running at 8% of sales.
Direct Labor Productivity	8,000,000	5%	400,000	
Purchase Cost Reduction	24,000,000	4%	960,000	
Inventory Reduction	18,000,000	20% at 15%	540,000	The inventory is projected to decrease by 20%. A carrying cost of 15% was used.
Obsolescence	250,000	20%	50,000	
Warranty Cost Reduction	400,000	25%	100,000	
Gross Annual Benefits			$2,370,000	
Subtracting: Recurring Costs			− 133,000	
Net Annual Benefits			$2,237,000	

	Divided by 12
Cost of a One-Month Delay	$186,416
Payback Period (one-time costs/(net annual benefits/12))	6.5 Months, Following Full Implementation
Return on Investment (net annual benefits/one-time costs)	185%

These are interesting numbers. First of all, they indicate the MRP II project will pay for itself in less than one year after full implementation, in fact, in just 6.5 months.

Secondly, the lost opportunity cost of a one-month delay is $186,000. This very powerful number should be made highly visible during the entire project, for several reasons:

1. It imparts a sense of urgency. ("We really do need to get MRP II implemented in eighteen months.")

2. It helps to establish priorities. ("This project really is the number two priority in the company.")

3. It puts the resource allocation issue into clearer focus.

Regarding this last point, think back to the concept of the "three knobs" from Chapter 2—*work* to be done, *time* available in which to do it, and *resources* which can be applied. Recall that any two of these elements can be held constant by varying the third.

Too often in the past, companies have assumed their only option is to increase the time. They assumed (often incorrectly) that both the workload and resources are fixed. The result of this assumption: a stretched out implementation, with its attendant decrease in the odds for success.

Making everyone aware of the cost of a one-month delay can help companies avoid that trap. BUT *the key people really must believe the numbers.* (More on this later.) For example, let's assume the company's in a bind on the MRP II project schedule. They're short of people in a key function. The choices are:

1. Delay the implementation for three months. Cost: $558,000 ($186,000 × 3).

2. Stay on schedule by getting temporary help from outside the company. Cost: $120,000.

No one will deny $120,000 is a lot of money. But it's a whole lot less than $558,000.

So far in this example, I've been talking about costs (expenses) and benefits (income). Cash flow is another important financial consideration, and there's good news and bad news here.

First, the bad news.

A company must spend virtually all of the $1.2 million (one-time costs) before getting anything back.

The good news.

Enormous amounts of cash are freed up, largely as a result of the inventory decrease. The cost justification for Company T projects an inventory reduction of $3.6 million (20 percent of $18 million). This represents incoming cash flow. See Figure 4-4 for details.

MRP II appears to be very attractive for Company T: an excellent return on investment (186%) and substantial amounts of cash being freed up.

How might a different kind of company come out of the cost

Figure 4-4 Company T Projected Cash Flow From MRP II

Year	Annual	Cumulative	
1	−$1,084,500	−$1,084,500	90% of One-Time Costs
2	−120,500		Balance (10%) of One-Time Costs
	−133,000		Annual Recurring Costs
	+1,185,000		50% of Gross Annual Benefits
	+900,000		25% of Inventory Reduction
	+$1,831,500	+$747,000	
3	−133,000		Annual Recurring Costs
	+1,830,000		Gross Annual Benefits
	+2,700,000		Balance (75%) of Inventory Reduction
	+$4,397,000	+$5,144,000	Total Cash Flow at end of Year 3

justification? For example, one that's larger, with more locations, and in a different industry? Well, let's see.

Here's a profile on another manufacturer, this one called Company P & R (for *Process* and *Repetitive*):

Annual Sales: $800,000,000

Employees: 3,000

Plants: 3

Distribution Centers: 8

Process: highly repetitive; many in-line operations; some flow processing

Product: consumer goods, make-to-stock

Net Profit % (pre-tax): 12%

Annual Direct Labor Cost: $20,000,000

Annual Purchase Volume: (Production Materials) $180,000,000

Current Inventories:

Manufacturing (includes raw materials, WIP, etc.): $30,000,000

Distribution (finished goods): $60,000,000

Company P & R's cost justification is shown in Figure 4-5. The company is larger than Company T and more geographically dispersed. Its products are simpler, but made in much greater volume and much faster. They have a network of eight distribution centers in place, and Distribution Resource Planning (DRP) will be required.

Figure 4-5 Company P & R Cost Justification

COSTS			
C-Computer	One-Time	Recurring	Comments
Hardware	$300,000	—	A hardware purchase, not lease.

C-Computer	One-Time	Recurring	Comments
Software	350,000	35,000	Includes purchase of DRP software. Software maintenance contract costs $35,000.
Systems and Programming	675,000	60,000	Included here is the internal development of a new forecasting and order entry system.

B-Data	One-Time	Recurring	Comments
Inventory Records	800,000	90,000	This will be a major effort, at the branch warehouses as well as the plants.
Bills of Material	50,000	—	The bills are simple and fairly accurate.
Routings	—	—	The routings are simple, and currently very accurate.
Forecasting	90,000	60,000	Marketing will need to add a full-time person for sales forecasting. That person will come on board early.

A-People	One-time	Recurring	Comments
Project Team	600,000	—	One full-time project leader at each plant, a corporate project leader and an assistant— all for two years.
Outside Education	250,000	25,000	
Inside Education	280,000	80,000	
Professional Guidance	90,000	2,000	
Total	$3,485,000	$352,000	

BENEFITS Function	Current	% Improvement	Annual Benefits	Comments
Sales	$800,000,000	0	—	The company's fill rate (% of orders shipped from stock) is already very high.

BENEFITS Function	Current	% Improvement	Annual Benefits	Comments
Direct Labor Productivity	20,000,000	7%	$1,400,000	Mainly through reductions in idle time, overtime, lay-off, and training. Costs caused by the lack of a good planning and scheduling system.
Purchase Cost	180,000,000	2%	3,600,000	
Inventories Manufacturing	30,000,000	10% @ 15%	450,000	
Distribution	60,000,000	25% @ 15%	2,250,000	
Obsolescence	—	—	—	
Quality	—	—	—	
Premium Freight	300,000	50%	150,000	Primarily outbound: from the plants to the branch warehouses and from the branches to the customers.

Other (elimination of annual physical inventory)		50,000
Gross Annual Benefits		$7,900,000
Subtracting: Recurring Cost		−352,000
Net Annual Benefits		$7,548,000

divided by 12

Cost of a One-Month Delay	$629,000
Payback Period	5.5 months
Return on Investment	216%

Company P & R plans on implementing all of MRP II in all plants within two years. DRP will be implemented simultaneously, as a part of basic MRP.

Implementing MRP II/DRP in Company P & R will be more complex and take longer in a smaller one-location organization like Company T. The rewards are proportionately greater; typically the larger the company, the more highly leveraged are the benefits from MRP II. However, even for a much smaller company, MRP II can represent a very solid investment.

Company S (for "Small") looks like this:

Annual Sales: $8,000,000

Employees: 150

Plants: 1

Process: Fabrication and assembly

Product: OEM components, make-to-order

Net Profit % (pre-tax): 10%

Annual Direct Labor Cost: $800,000

Annual Purchase Volume: $2,400,000

Current Inventories: $1,800,000

See Figure 4-6 for Company S's cost justification. The bad news: benefits from MRP II are less highly leveraged in smaller companies.

The good news: even in a small company, MRP II is a super investment.

Figure 4-6 Company S Cost Justification

COSTS C-Computer	One-Time	Recurring	Comments
Hardware and Software	$100,000	$5,000	Company S has no computer. This covers the purchase of a microcomputer and software with a $5,000 per year maintenance contract.
Systems and Programming	45,000	36,000	This reflects the hiring of a data processing person to operate the computer, install the software, make additions to it, etc.

B-Data	One-Time	Recurring	Comments
Inventory Records	65,000	15,000	One-time costs are equipment and people. Recurring costs cover a half-time cycle counter.
Bills of Material	—	—	The small amount of work needed to get bill accuracy will be done by people on the exempt payroll.
Routings	100,000	15,000	Company S has no routings and no standards. An outside industrial engineering firm will be used to help create the routings and standards, and a halftime person will be required to maintain them.

A-People	One-Time	Recurring	Comments
Project Team	56,250	—	
Outside Education	30,000	3,000	
Inside Education	30,000	6,000	
Professional Guidance	18,000	2,000	
Total	$444,250	$82,000	

BENEFITS Function	Current	% Improvement	Annual Benefits
Sales	$8,000,000	10% @ 10%	$80,000
Direct Labor Productivity	800,000	10%	80,000
Purchase Cost	2,400,000	3%	72,000
Inventories	1,800,000	30% @ 20%	108,000
Obsolescence	150,000	50%	75,000
Quality (scrap)	200,000	50%	100,000
Premium freight	50,000	50%	25,000
Other	—	—	—
Gross Annual Benefits			$540,000
Subtracting: Recurring Costs			−80,000

BENEFITS Function	Current	% Improvement	Annual Benefits
Net Annual Benefits			$460,000
	divided by 12		
Cost of One Month-Delay			$38,333
Payback Period			11.6 months
RETURN ON INVESTMENT			104%

Here are a few final thoughts on cost justification.

1. What I've been trying to illustrate here is primarily the *process* of cost justification, not how to format the numbers. Use whatever format the corporate office requires.

2. I've dealt mostly with out-of-pocket costs. For example, the opportunity costs of the managers' time have not been applied to the project, because these people are on the exempt payroll and have a job to do, regardless of how many hours will be involved. Some companies don't do it that way. They include the estimated costs of management's time, in order to decide on the relative merits of competing projects. This is also a valid approach, and should be followed in companies doing it that way.

3. Get widespread participation in the cost justification process. Have all of the key departments involved. Avoid the trap of cost justifying the entire project on the basis of inventory reduction alone. It's probably possible to do it that way and come up with the necessary payback and return on investment numbers. Unfortunately, it sends exactly the wrong message to the rest of the company. It says: "This is an inventory reduction project," and that's wrong. MRP II is a whole lot more than that.

4. To keep the examples as uncluttered as possible, I didn't add in any costs for contingency. Some companies prefer to include in the cost justification some dollars for unanticipated expenses. Their rationale is that if a "surprise" occurs, money is already in the budget to solve the problem. If there are no "surprises," then, of course, the money isn't spent.

5. Some companies have received substantial benefits quite early in the implementation process. This can happen as a result of implementing production planning, getting the inventory records accurate, upgrading the bills and routings, etc. This is fine when it occurs, but I recommend against trying to express this in the cost justification. Doing so may result in undue pressure for early payback, at a time when the people have their hands full running the business with today's tools and implementing the superior set of tools called MRP II.

6. A few companies, usually very small and growing rapidly, have a difficult time cost justifying MRP II based on improvements to their *current* mode of operation. Because of their small size, the lack of effective formal systems isn't a major hindrance. However, they know that their rapid growth will soon get them to a size where the informal systems will begin to break down. The answer, they believe, is MRP II. But how can they justify it based on dollars and cents? What will be the benefits?

One approach is to project how large the company will be at some point in the future, based on anticipated growth rates, and to estimate the penalties of having to operate in that environment with today's systems. These penalties would be the costs from poor customer service, low productivity, poor purchase cost performance, excessive inventories, scrap, obsolescence, etc. The elimination of these costs can become the benefit numbers in the cost justification equation.

Commitment

Getting commitment is the first "moment of truth" in an implementation project. This is when the company turns thumbs up or thumbs down on MRP II. See Figure 4-7.

As a result of First-Cut Education and going through the cost justification, the key top management and operating management people should now know:

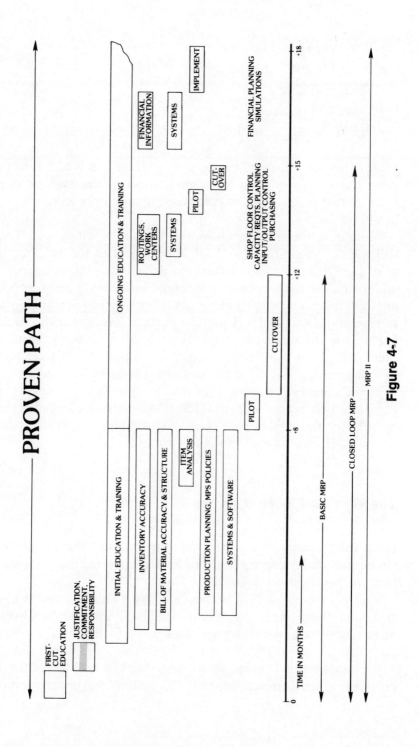

Figure 4-7

- What is MRP II?
- Is it right for our company?
- What will it cost?
- What will it save?
- Are we ready to do it?

How do the numbers in the cost justification look? Are they good enough to peg the implementation of the system as the number two priority in the company, second only to running the business?

Sometimes the numbers look solid and compelling, but it may still not be possible to establish the project as the number two priority. Other very time-consuming activities may already be underway, such as building a new plant, introducing a new product line, entering a new market, or absorbing an acquired company. Everything about MRP II may be perfect, except for the timing.

If this is the case, put MRP II on hold for a while until that other very time-consuming activity is completed. It's far better to delay getting started than to make a false start.

There's one final acid test for implementation readiness: Is the company prepared to keep MRP II as the overall number two priority for the next several years? If the answer is "No," don't go ahead. If it's "Yes," put it in *writing*.

The Written Project Charter

Do a formal sign-off on the cost justification. The people who developed and accepted the numbers should put their names on the cost justification document.

That document should be prefaced by a charter, which might read something like: "We, the undersigned, commit ourselves to achieving these benefits, within these costs, within this time frame, etc . . ."

Why make this process so formal? First, it will stress the importance of the project. Second, the written charter can serve as a beacon, a touchstone, a rallying point during the next eighteen months when (not if) the tough times come. Business may get real good, or real bad. Or the government gets on the company's back. Or, perhaps most frightening of all, the MRP II-knowledgeable and enthusiastic general manager is transferred to another division. His successor may not share his perspective on MRP II.

A written charter won't make these problems disappear. It *will* make it easier to address them, and to "stay the course."

We've just completed steps one and two on the *Proven Path:* First-Cut Education, and Cost Justification and Commitment. A company at this point has accomplished a number of things. First of all, its key people have received some education on MRP II. Secondly, they've estimated costs and benefits. Next, they've made a commitment to implement MRP II, via the *Proven Path* so that the company can get to Class A quickly.

The Implementers' Checklists

At this point, it's time to introduce the concept of Implementers' Checklists. These are documents which detail the major tasks necessary to ensure total compliance with the *Proven Path* approach.

A company which is able to check "Yes" for each task on each list can be virtually guaranteed of a successful implementation of MRP II. As such, therefore, these checklists can be important tools for key implementers—people like project leaders, torchbearers, general managers, and other members of the steering committee and project team.

Beginning here, an Implementers' Checklist will appear at the end of each chapter. The reader may be able to expand their utility by adding tasks, as appropriate. However, I recommend against the deletion of tasks from any of the checklists. To do so would weaken their ability to help monitor compliance with the *Proven Path*.

IMPLEMENTERS' CHECKLIST

Function: COST JUSTIFICATION & COMMITMENT

TASK	Complete Yes	No
1. The general manager and key staff members have attended First-Cut Education.	____	____
2. All key operating managers (department heads) have attended First-Cut Education.	____	____
3. Cost justification prepared on a joint basis, with both top management and operating management from all involved functions participating.	____	____
4. Cost justification approved by general manager and all other necessary individuals.	____	____
5. Manufacturing Resource Planning established as the company's number two priority.	____	____
6. Written project charter created and formally signed off by all executives and managers participating in the justification process.	____	____

Project Organization and Responsibilities

Once a commitment to implement MRP II is made, it's time to get organized for the project. Some new groups will need to be created, as well as one or more temporary positions.

Project Leader

The project leader is the key person who will head up the MRP II project team, and spearhead the implementation at the operational level. Let's examine some of the requirements of this position.

Requirement #1: The project leader must be full-time. Having a full-time project leader is one of the ways to break through the "Catch-22," as discussed in Chapter 2, and get to Class A within two years.

Except in very small companies (those with about 100 or fewer employees), it's essential to free a key person from all operational responsibilities. If this doesn't happen, that part-time project leader/part-time operating person will often have to spend time on Priority #1 (running the business) at the expense of Priority #2 (making progress on MRP II). The result: delays, a stretched out implementation, and sharply reduced odds for success.

Requirement #2: The project leader should be an insider, someone from within the company. Resist the temptation to hire an "MRP II expert" from outside to be the project leader. There are several important reasons:

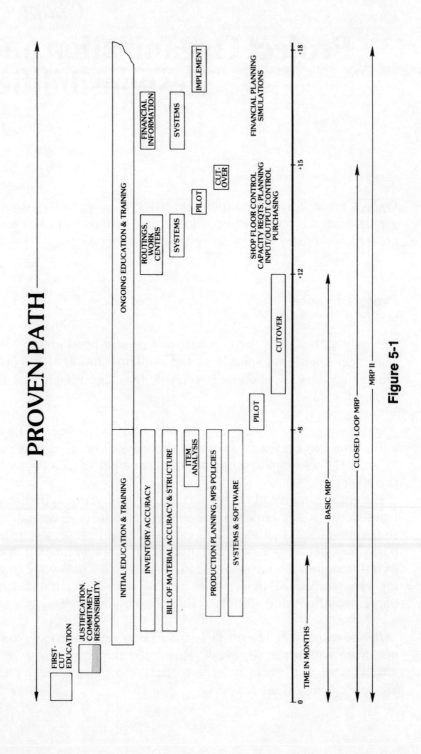

Figure 5-1

1. MRP II isn't complicated. It won't take long for the "insider" to learn all he needs to know about MRP II—even though that person may have no background in materials management, data processing, etc.

2. It will take the "outsider" (a project leader from outside the company who knows MRP II) far longer to learn about the company: its *products,* its *processes,* and its *people.* The project leader must know these things, because implementing MRP II successfully means changing the way the business will be run. This requires knowing how the business is being run today.

3. While it will take a long time for the outsider to learn the products, the processes, and the people—it will take even longer for the *people to "learn" the project leader.* The outside expert brings with him little credibility, little trust, and probably little rapport. He may be a terrific person, but is fundamentally an *unknown quantity* to the people inside the company.

4. This approach can often result in the "insiders" sitting back, reluctant to get involved, and prepared to watch the new guy "do a wheelie." Their attitude: "MRP II? Oh. That's Charlie's job. He's that new guy the company hired to install MRP II. He's taking care of that." This results in MRP II no longer being an operational effort to change the way the business is run. Rather it becomes another systems project headed up by an outsider, and the odds for success drop sharply.

Requirement #3: The project leader should have an operational background. He should come from an operating department within the company—a department involved in a key function regarding the products: design, sales, production, purchasing, planning. I recommend against selecting the project leader from the data processing department, unless that person also has recent, meaningful operating experience within the company.

One reason is that, typically, a data processing person hasn't been directly involved in the challenging business of getting product shipped, week after week, month after month. He hasn't "been there," even though he may have been working longer hours than the operational folks. Another problem with selecting a data processing person to head up the entire project is that it sends the wrong signal throughout the company. It says: "This is a computer project." Obviously it's not. It's a line management activity, involving virtually all areas of the business.

Requirement #4: The project leader should be the best available person for the job from within the ranks of the operating managers of the business—the department heads. Bite the bullet, and relieve the best middle manager from all operating responsibilities, and appoint him project leader. It's that important.

In any given company, there's a wide variety of candidates:

Production Manager

Purchasing Manager

Sales Administration Manager

Production & Inventory Control Manager

Customer Service Manager

Product Engineering Manager

Manufacturing Engineering Manager

Materials Manager

Distribution Manager

One of the "best-background" project leaders I've ever seen was in a machine tool company. Their project leader had been the *assembly superintendent.* Of all the people in a typical machine tool company, perhaps the assembly superintendent understands the problems best. (Assembly superintendents are often heard to say things like: "We don't have the parts. Give us the parts and we'll make the product." They tend to say this with greater frequency and volume near the end of the month.)

Often, senior executives are reluctant to assign that really excellent operating manager totally to MRP II. While they realize the critical importance of MRP II and the need for a "heavyweight" to manage it, they're hesitant. Perhaps they're concerned, understandably, about the impact on Priority #1 (running the business).

Imagine the following conversation between a general manager and myself:

GENERAL MANAGER (GM): We can't afford to free up any of our operating managers to be the full-time project leader. We just don't have enough management depth. We'll have to hire the project leader from outside.

TOM WALLACE (TW): Oh really? Suppose one of your key managers was to get run over by a train tomorrow. Are you telling me that your company would be in big trouble?

GM: Oh no, not at all.

TW: What would you do in that case?

GM: We'd have to hire the replacement from outside the company. As I said, we don't have much bench strength.

TW: Great. Make believe your best manager just got run over by a train. Make him the full-time project leader. Fill the vacated job with an outside hire, if necessary.

Requirement #5: The project leader should be a veteran—someone who's been with the company for a good while, and has the scar tissue to prove it. People who are quite new to the company are still technically "outsiders." They don't know the business, or the people. The people don't know them; trust hasn't had time to develop. Companies, other than very young ones, should try to get as their project leader someone who's been on board for at least five years or so.

Requirement #6: The project leader should have good people skills, good communication skills, the respect and trust of his peers, and a good track record. In short, someone who's a good person and a good manager. It's important, because the project leader's job is almost entirely involved with people. The important elements are things like trust, mutual respect, frequent and open communications, and enthusiasm.

See Figure 5-2 for a summary of the characteristics of the project leader.

What does the project leader do? Quite a bit, and I'll discuss some of the details later, after examining the other elements of organization for MRP II. For the time being, however, please refer to Figure 5-3 for an outline of the job.

Figure 5-2 Project Leader Characteristics

- full-time on the project.
- assigned from within the company, not hired from outside.
- an operating person—someone who has been deeply involved in making shipments and/or other fundamental aspects of running the business.
- heavyweight, not a lightweight.
- a veteran with the company, not a rookie.
- a good manager and a respected person within the company.

Project Team

The next step in getting organized is to establish the MRP II project team. This is the group responsible for implementing the system at the operational level. Its jobs include:

- establishing the MRP II project schedule.
- reporting actual performance against the schedule.
- identifying problems and obstacles to successful implementation.
- activating "ad hoc" groups called "spin-off task forces" (discussed later in this chapter) to solve these problems.
- making decisions, as appropriate, regarding priorities, resource reallocation, etc.
- making recommendations, when necessary, to the "executive steering committee" (discussed later in this chapter).
- doing whatever is required to permit a smooth, rapid and

Figure 5-3 Project Leader Job Outline

- chairs the MRP II project team.
- is a member of the MRP II executive steering committee.
- oversees the MRP II educational process—both outside and inside.
- coordinates the preparation of the MRP II project schedule, obtaining concurrence and commitment from all involved parties.
- updates the project schedule each week and highlights jobs behind schedule.
- counsels with departments and individuals who are behind schedule, and attempts to help them get back on schedule.
- reports serious behind-schedule situations to the executive steering committee, and makes recommendations for their solution.
- reschedules the project as necessary and only when directed by the executive steering committee.
- works closely with the outside consultant, routinely keeping that person advised of progress and problems.

The essence of the project leader's job is to remove obstacles and to support the people doing the work of implementing MRP II:

• the foremen	• the programmers
• the buyers	• the marketing people
• the engineers	• the stockroom
• the planners	• the executives
• the accountants	• etc.

successful implementation of MRP II at the operational level of the business.

The project team consists of relatively few full-time members. This would include the project leader, perhaps one or several assistant project leaders (to support the project leader, coordinate education, write procedures, provide support to other departments, etc.), and often one or more data processing people involved full-time in the project.

Most of the members of the project team are part-time members. They are the department heads—the operating managers of the business. Below is an example of a project team from sample Company T (as described in Chapter 4—800 people, one location, fabrication and assembly, make-to-order product, etc.).

Full-Time Members	*Part-Time Members*
Project Leader	Cost Accounting Manager
Assistant Project Leader	Data Processing Manager
Systems Analyst	General Accounting Manager
Programmers (2)	Manufacturing Engineering Manager
	Personnel Manager
	Plant Manager
	Product Engineering Manager
	Production Control Manager
	Purchasing Manager
	Quality Control Manager
	Sales Administration Manager

This group adds up to a total of sixteen people, which is big enough to handle the job but certainly not too large to execute their responsibilities effectively.

The project team meets once or twice per week for about an hour. When done properly, meetings are crisp and to the point. A typical meeting would consist of:

1. Feedback on the status of the project schedule—what tasks have been completed in the past week, what tasks have been started in the past week, what's behind schedule.

2. A review of an interim report from a task force which has been addressing a specific problem.

3. A decision on the priority of a requested enhancement to the software.

4. Identification of a potential (or real) problem. Perhaps the creation of another task force to address the problem.

Please note—no education is being done here, no consensus building, no getting into the nitty gritty. These things are all essential, but should be done in sessions other than the full project team meetings.

The moral: keep 'em brief. Remember, the managers still have a business to run—plus other things to do to get MRP II implemented.

UPWARD DELEGATION

Brevity is one important characteristic of the project team meetings. Another is that they be mandatory. The members of the project team need to attend each meeting.

Except . . . what about Priority #1? What about running the business? Situations just might arise when it's more important for a manager to be somewhere else. For example, the plant manager may be needed on the plant floor to solve a critical production problem; the customer service manager may need to meet with a very important new customer who's come in to see the shop; the purchasing manager may have to visit a problem vendor who's supplying some critical items.

Some companies have used a technique called "upward delegation" very effectively. If, at any time, a given project team member has a higher priority than attending a project team meeting, that's fine. No problem. All he has to do is make certain his designated alternate will be there in his place. Who's the designated alternate? It's his boss . . . the vice president of manufacturing, or marketing, or materials per the above examples. The boss covers for the department head. In this way, Priority #1 is taken care of while keeping the project team meetings populated by people who can make decisions.

The Executive Steering Committee

The executive steering committee consists primarily of the top management group in the company. Its mission is to *ensure* a successful implementation. The project leader cannot do this; the project team can't; only the top management group can ensure success.

To do this, the executive steering committee meets once or twice a month for about an hour. Its members include the general manager, the vice presidents, and one additional person—the full-time project leader. The project leader acts as the link between the executive steering committee and the project team.

The main order of business at the steering committee meetings is a review of the status of the project. It's the project leader's responsibility to report progress relative to the schedule, specifically where they're behind. He explains the seriousness of schedule delays, reviews tasks on the critical path, outlines plans to get the project back on schedule, identifies additional resources required, etc.

The steering committee's job is to review these situations and make the tough decisions. In the case of a serious schedule slippage on the critical path, the steering committee needs to consider the following questions (not necessarily in the sequence listed):

- Can resources already existing within the company be reallocated and applied to the project? (Remember the "three knobs" principle discussed in Chapter 2? This represents turning up the resource knob.)
- Is it possible to acquire additional resources from outside the company? (The resource knob.) If so, how much will that cost versus the cost of a number of months of delay?
- Is all of the work called for by the project schedule really necessary? Would it be possible to reduce somewhat the amount of work without harming the chances for success with MRP II? (The work knob.)
- Will it be necessary to reschedule a portion of the project or, worst case, the entire project? (The time knob.)

In addition to schedule slippage, the executive steering committee may have to address other difficult issues: unforeseen obstacles, problem individuals in key positions, difficulties with the software vendor, etc.

Only the executive steering committee can authorize a delay in the project. These are the only people with the visibility, the control and the leverage to make such a decision. They are ultimately accountable.

The Torchbearer

The term "torchbearer" is used here in a very specific sense. It refers to the person with assigned *executive level* responsibility for MRP II. The torchbearer's role is to be the top management focal point for the entire project. Typically, he chairs the meetings of the executive steering committee.

Who should be the torchbearer? Ideally, and all things being equal, the general manager. After that, take your pick from any of the vice presidents. Most often, it's the VP of finance or the VP of manufacturing. The key ingredients are enthusiasm for MRP II and a willingness to devote some additional time to it.

Often, the project leader will be assigned to report directly to the torchbearer. This could happen despite a different reporting relationship prior to the MRP II project. For example, the project leader may have been the customer service manager and, as such, had reported to the VP of marketing. Now, as project leader, he reports to the torchbearer, who is the general manager, or perhaps the VP of finance.

What else does the torchbearer do? He "shows the top management flag," serves as an executive sounding board for the project team, and perhaps provides some top level muscle in dealings with suppliers. He rallies support from other executives as required.

Being a torchbearer isn't a terribly time-consuming function, but it can be very, very important. The best person for the job, almost invariably, is the general manager.

Spin-off Task Forces

Spin-off task forces are the ad hoc groups I referred to earlier. They represent a key tool to keep the project team from getting bogged down in a lot of detail.

A spin-off task force is typically created to address a specific issue. The issue could be relatively major (e.g., software selection, structuring modular bills of material, deciding how to master schedule satellite plants), or fairly minor (floor stock inventory control, engineering change procedures, etc.). The spin-off task force is given a specific amount of time—a week or so for a lesser issue, perhaps a bit longer for those more significant—to research the issue, formulate alternative solutions, and report back to the project team with recommendations.

Spin-off task forces:

- are created by the project team.
- are temporary.
- involve relatively few members of the project team (usually only one, as task force chairperson).
- are broad-based, normally involving people from more than one department.
- make their recommendations to the project team, then go out of existence.

Upon receiving a spin-off task force's report, the project team may:

- accept the task force's recommended solution.
- adopt one of the different alternatives identified by the task force.
- forward the matter to the executive steering committee, *with a recommendation.*
- disagree with the task force's report, and reactivate the task force with additional instructions.

Once the decision is made as to what to do, then people must be assigned to do it. This may include one or more members of the spin-off task force, or it may not. The task force's job is to *identify* the solution; it may be someone else's job to *implement* it.

Back in Chapter 3, I discussed "time wasters" such as documenting the current system or designing the new system. The organizational format which I'm recommending here—executive steering committee, project team and spin-off task forces—will do a far better job of ensuring that the details of MRP II will fit the business.

George Bevis, former senior vice president and torchbearer at the Tennant Company, coined the term "spin-off task force." He utilized the concept very successfully during Tennant's Class A implementation. George says, "Spin-off task forces work so well it's almost immoral."

Professional Guidance

MRP II is not an extension of past experience. For those who've never done it before, it's a whole new ball game. And most companies don't have anyone on board who has ever done it before—successfully.

Companies implementing MRP II need to get some help from an *experienced, qualified* professional in the field. They're sailing into uncharted (for them) waters; they need a pilot to guide them around the rocks and shoals. They need access to someone who's "been there."

Note the use of the words "experienced" and "qualified" in the prior paragraph. This refers to *meaningful Class A* experience. The key question is: Where has this person made it work? Has this person been involved in a Class A implementation in a significant way? Has this person truly "been there?"

Some companies recognize the need for professional guidance, but make the mistake of retaining someone without Class A credentials. They're no better off than before, because they're receiving advice on how to do it from a person who has not yet done it successfully.

Before deciding on a specific consultant, find out where he got his Class A experience. Then contact the company or companies given as references and establish:

1. Are they Class A?

2. Did the prospective consultant serve in a key role in the implementation?

If the answer to either question is "No," then run, don't walk, the other way! Find someone who has Class A experience. To do otherwise means that the company will be paying the "inexperienced" outsider (to get on-the-job training) and, at the same time, won't be getting the expert advice it needs so badly.

The consultant supports the general manager, the torchbearer (if other than the GM), the project leader, and other members of the executive steering committee and the project team. In addition to giving advice on specific issues, the outside professional also:

- asks questions which force people to address the tough issues. Example: "Are your inventories really 95% accurate overall? What about the floor stock? How about your work-in-process counts? How good are your shop order close-out procedures?"

- helps people focus on the right priorities and, hence, keep the project on the right track. Example: "I'm concerned about the sequence of some of the tasks on your project schedule. It seems to me that, in some cases, the cart may be ahead of the horse. Let's take a look."

- serves as a sounding board, perhaps helping to resolve issues of disagreement among several people or groups.

- serves as a "conscience" to top management (addressing, when necessary, issues too difficult for other people in the company to raise).

What the consultant should *not* do is write procedures, draw flow charts, write job descriptions, develop computer program specifications and so on. Unfortunately, many consulting firms out there do exactly those kinds of things. Most large consulting organizations—be they a conventional consulting company, the management services division of a CPA firm, or the consulting group within a software vendor—have as their objective to maximize billable days.

This is in direct conflict with the company's objective of implementing MRP II successfully. Pouring on lots of consulting is the wrong way to do it. A little bit of consulting, of the right kind, can often make the difference between success and failure. A great deal of consulting, of whatever quality, is almost always counterproductive to a successful implementation.

Why? Because the consultants "take over" to one degree or another. They become deeply involved in the implementation process. And that's exactly the wrong way to do it. It inhibits the development of the essential ingredients for success: user understanding, a willingness to change the way they do their jobs, "ownership" of the system, and line accountability for results.

How much consulting is the right amount? How often should you see your consultant?

Answer: no more than one or two days every month or two. Perhaps a two-day visit to get started, then, on average, a day every six weeks.

What happens during those one-day visits?

Answer: A typical consulting day could take this format:

8:30	Preliminary meeting with general manager, torchbearer and project leader.
9:00–10:00	Project team meeting
10:00–3:00	Meetings with individuals and smaller groups to focus on specific issues.
3:00–3:30	"Solitary time" for consultant to review notes, collect thoughts, formulate recommendations, etc.

3:30–4:30   Executive steering committee meeting. Consultant updates members on his findings, recommendations, etc.

In between visits, the consultant must be easily reachable by telephone. The consultant needs to be a *routinely available* resource for information and recommendations . . . but visits the plant in person only once each month or two.

The MRP Project Schedule

The MRP II project schedule is the basic control tool used to manage the project to a timely and successful conclusion. It needs to be:

- Aggressive but attainable, i.e., an "eighteen-month" schedule.
- Expressed in days or weeks, for at least the short- and medium-term. Just as with MRP II itself, months are too large a time frame for effective scheduling.
- Complete, covering all the tasks through Closing the Loop and Finance & Simulation.
- In sufficient detail to manage the project effectively, but not so weighty it overwhelms the people using it.
- Specific in assigning accountability. It should name names, not merely job titles and/or departments.

Creating the Project Schedule. There needs to be a widespread "buy-in" to the project schedule. If not, it'll be just another piece of paper. It follows, then, that the people who develop the project schedule need to be the same people who'll be held accountable for sticking to it. They're primarily the department managers, and they're on the project team.

The project leader can help the department heads (and other project team members) develop the project schedule. However, he cannot do it for them, or dictate to them what will be done and when.

Here's one good way to approach it:

1. Each member of the project team reviews Darryl Landvater's Detailed Implementation Plan individually (see Appendix C). In this process, they need to add and delete steps where necessary, assign people, make estimates of time, etc.

2. This information goes to the project leader, who puts it together into a first-cut schedule.

3. This first-cut schedule is given to the project team members for their review, adjustment, etc. During this process, they may wish to consult with their bosses, most of whom are on the executive steering committee.

4. The project team finalizes the project schedule.

5. The project leader presents the schedule to the executive steering committee for their approval.

A process such as this helps to generate consensus, commitment, and willingness to work hard to hit the schedule.

Managing the Schedule—A Scenario

Consider the following case, a typical example of what could occur in practically any company implementing MRP II using the *Proven Path*. The project leader (PL) is talking to the manufacturing engineering manager (ME).

PL: Mike, we've got a problem. Your department is three weeks late on the MRP II project schedule, specifically routing accuracy.

ME: I know we are, Pat, and I really don't know what to do about it. We've got all that new equipment coming in back in Department 15, and all of my people are tied up on that project.

(Author's Comment: This is possibly a case of conflict between Priority #2—implement MRP II—and Priority #1—run the business.)

PL: Can I help?

ME: Thanks, Pat, but I don't think so. I'll have to talk to my boss. What's the impact of us being behind?

PL: With this one, we're on the critical path for shop floor control. Each week late means a one-week delay in the overall implementation of MRP II.

ME: Ouch, that smarts. When's the next steering committee meeting?

(Author's Comment: Mike knows Pat and the other members of the executive steering committee will be meeting shortly to review performance to the project schedule.)

PL: Next Tuesday.

ME: OK. I'll get back to you.

PL: Fine. Remember, if I can help out in any way . . .

At this point, from the project leader's point of view, the matter is well on the way to resolution. Here's why:

1. Mike, the manufacturing engineering manager, knows his department's schedule slippage will be reported at the executive steering committee meeting. (Pat, the project leader, has no choice but to report it; that's part of her job.)

2. Mike knows that his boss, the VP of manufacturing, will be in that meeting along with his boss's boss, the general manager.

3. Mike knows his boss doesn't like "surprises" of this type (who does?).

4. Unless Mike likes to play Russian roulette with his career, he'll get together with his boss *prior to* the steering committee meeting.

When they meet, they'll discuss how to get back on schedule, identifying alternatives, costs, etc. They may be able to solve the problem themselves. On the other hand, the only possible solution may be expensive, and require higher level approval. In that case, the executive steering committee would be the appropriate forum.

Or, worst case, there may be no feasible solution at all. That's when it becomes bullet-biting time for the steering committee. That group, and only that group, authorizes a reschedule of the MRP II project.

One last point before leaving Pat and Mike. Note the project leader's approach: "*We* have a problem," "Can I help?", "*We're* on the critical path," etc. One of Robert Townsend's remarks on managers in general certainly applies to MRP II project leaders— a large part of their job is to facilitate, to carry the water bucket[1] for the folks doing the work.

[1] Robert Townsend, *Up the Organization* (New York: Alfred A. Knopf, 1978), p. 11.

IMPLEMENTERS' CHECKLIST

Function: PROJECT ORGANIZATION AND RESPONSIBILITIES

Task	Complete Yes	No
1. Full-time project leader selected from a key management role in an operating department within the company.	____	____
2. Torchbearer identified and formally appointed.	____	____
3. Project team formed, consisting mainly of operating managers of all involved departments.	____	____
4. Executive steering committee formed, consisting of the general manager, all staff members, and the project leader.	____	____
5. Project team meeting at least once per week.	____	____
6. Executive steering committee meeting at least once per month.	____	____
7. Outside counsel, with Class A MRP II experience, retained and on site no more than one or two days every month or two.	____	____
8. Detailed project schedule established by the project team, naming names, in days or weeks, and showing completion of MRP II project in less than two years.	____	____
9. Detailed project schedule being updated at least weekly at project team meetings, with status being reported at each meeting of the executive steering committee.	____	____

Chapter 6

Education Makes the Difference

It's fascinating to look back on how education for MRP and MRP II has been viewed over the last twenty-five years. Quite an evolution has taken place.

At the beginning, in what could be called the *Dark Ages,* education of any kind wasn't perceived as necessary. The implication was that the users would figure it out on the fly. The relatively few early successes were, not surprisingly, in companies where the users were deeply involved in the design of the system and, hence, became educated as part of that process.

The Dark Ages were followed by the *How Not Why* era. Attention was focused on telling people *how* to do things, but not *why* certain things needed to be done. This approach may possibly work in certain parts of the world, but its track record in North America proved to be poor indeed.

Next came the age of *Give 'Em the Facts.* With it came the recognition that people needed to see the "big picture," that they needed to understand the principles and concepts as well as the mechanics.

Was this new awareness a step forward? Yes. Did it help to improve the success rate? You bet. Was it the total answer? Not by a long shot.

Objectives of Education for MRP II

Today, education for MRP II is seen as having a far broader mission. It's recognized as having not one but two critically important objectives:

Fact Transfer. This takes place when people learn the "what's, why's and how's." It's essential, but by itself, it's not nearly enough.

Behavior Change. This occurs when people who have lived in the world of the informal system *become convinced of the need to do their jobs differently.* It's when they truly understand why and how they should use a formal system as a team to run the business more professionally, and how it will benefit them.

Some examples. *Fact transfer* occurs when the marketing people learn about the master schedule, how it should be used as the source of customer order promising, how to calculate the available-to-promise quantity.

Behavior change takes place when the marketing folks participate willingly in the sales forecasting and master scheduling process, because they recognize it as the way to give better and faster service to their customers, increase sales volume, and make the company more competitive.

Fact transfer happens when the production manager learns about shop floor control and how the dispatch list can be used by foremen to manage their departments more efficiently. *Behavior change* is when the production manager banishes hot lists from the plant floor, because he's convinced that the formal system can and will work.

Fact transfer is the engineers learning about the engineering change control capabilities within material requirements planning. *Behavior change* is the engineers communicating early and often with material planners about new products and pending engineering changes, because they understand how this will help drastically reduce obsolescence, disruptions to production, and late shipments to customers.

Behavior change is central to a successful implementation of Manufacturing Resource Planning. It's also an awesome task— *to enable hundreds or perhaps thousands of people to change the way they do their jobs.*

The mission of the MRP II education program is, therefore, of enormous importance. It involves not only fact transfer, by itself not a small task but, far more important, behavior change. One can speculate about the odds for success for the company using an off-the-wall, half-baked approach to education.

A key element in the *Proven Path,* perhaps the most important of all, is doing education, and doing it effectively. Doing education effectively is synonymous with *managing the process of change.* Behavior change is a *process* which people work through. In so doing, they come to believe in this new set of tools, this new set of values, this new way of managing a manufacturing company. Further, they acquire *ownership* of it. It becomes theirs; it becomes "the way we're going to run the business." Executing the process of behavior change, i.e., education for MRP II, is a *management* issue, not a technical one. The results of this process are teams of people who believe in this new way to run the business, and who are prepared to change the way they do their jobs to make it happen.

Criteria for a Program to Accomplish Behavior Change

Following are the criteria for this process, for an MRP II education program that will achieve the primary objective of behavior change widely throughout the company. (See Figure 6-1 for a summary of these criteria.)

1. *Active top management leadership and participation in the education process.* The need to involve top management deeply

Figure 6-1 Criteria for a Program to Accomplish Behavior Change

1. Active top management leadership and participation in the education process.
2. Line accountability for education.
3. Total immersion for key people.
4. Total coverage throughout the company.
5. Continuing reinforcement.
6. Instructor credibility.
7. Peer confirmation.
8. Enthusiasm.

in this change process is absolute. This group is the most important of all, and within this group, the general manager is the most important person. Failure to educate top management, and most specifically the general manager, is probably the single most significant cause of companies not succeeding with MRP II. Why? For several reasons, one being the law of organizational gravity. Change must cascade down the organization chart; it doesn't flow uphill.

Another reason: the risk factor. How could a company possibly succeed in acquiring a superior set of tools to manage the business, when the senior managers of the business don't understand the tools and how to use them? One well-intentioned decision by an uninformed general manager can kill an otherwise solid MRP II system. An example: the general manager says "Business is great! Put all of those new orders into the master schedule. So what if it gets overloaded? That'll motivate the troops." There goes the integrity of the master production schedule, and hence, the effectiveness of MRP II.

Another example: "Business is lousy! We have to cut indirect payroll expense. Lay off the cycle counter." There goes the integrity of the inventory records, and hence, the effectiveness of MRP II.

Okay so far? Now the next question to address is how to convince top management, specifically the general manager, to get educated. In some companies, this is no problem. The GM is open-minded, and more than willing to take several days out of a busy schedule to go to a class on MRP II.

In some companies, unfortunately, this is not so. The GM is unwilling to take the time to know about MRP II. Common objections:

"I don't need to know that. That's for the guys and gals in the back room."

"I know it all already. I went to a seminar by our computer hardware supplier three years ago."

"I'll support the system. I'm committed. I'll sign the appropriations requests. I don't need to do any more than that."

(Author's note: "Support" isn't good enough. Neither is "commitment." What's absolutely necessary is *informed* leadership by the general manager. Note the use of the word "informed"; this comes about through education.)

"I'm too busy."

And on and on. The reluctance by GMs to get educated most often falls into one of two categories:

Lack of understanding (they either think they know all about it, or they don't think they need to know about it at all), or secondly,

Lack of comfort with the notion of needing education.

The first category—lack of understanding—can usually be addressed by logic. Articles, books, videotapes, oral presentations have all been used with success. Perhaps the most effective approach is what's called an "executive briefing." This is a presentation by a qualified MRP II professional, lasting for several hours, to the general manager and his staff. This is not education, but rather an introduction to MRP II. The mission: for the general manager and staff to see the connection between the company's goals and the set of tools called MRP II, and to understand how MRP II can assist the company in reaching those goals and objectives (increased sales, reduced costs, better product quality, improved quality of life, enhanced ability to cope with change, etc.). It can then become much easier for the GM to see the real need to learn about MRP II, in order to make an informed decision about this potentially very important issue.

The second category—discomfort with the education process—is often not amenable to logic. It's emotional, and can run deep. Here are three ways which have been successful:

a. *Peer input.* Put the reluctant general manager in touch with other GMs who have been through both MRP II education and a successful implementation. Their input can often be sufficiently reassuring to defuse the issue.

b. *The Trusted Lieutenant.* Send one or several of the reluctant general manager's most trusted vice presidents to a top management MRP II class. Hopefully, their subsequent recommendation will be something like this: "Boss, you have to get some education on MRP II if we're going to make this thing work. Take our word for it—we can't do it without you."

c. *The Safety Glasses Approach.* Imagine this dialogue between the reluctant general manager and another person, perhaps the torchbearer.

TORCHBEARER (TB): Boss, when you go out on the plant floor, do you wear safety glasses?

GENERAL MANAGER (GM): Of course.

TB: Why? Are you afraid of getting metal in your eye?

GM (chuckling): No, of course not. I don't get my head that close to the machinery. The reason I wear safety glasses on the plant floor is that to do otherwise would send out the wrong signal. It would say that wearing safety glasses wasn't important. It would make it difficult for the managers and supervisors to enforce the rule that everyone must wear safety glasses.

TB: Well, boss, what kind of signal are you going to send out if you refuse to go through the MRP II education? We'll be asking many of our people to devote many of their hours to getting educated on MRP II. Without you setting the example, that'll be a whole lot harder.

Again the best way overall to resolve the issue of top management education is via the executive briefing. Address the issues up front, get agreement to go through the First-Cut Education process correctly, then do the cost justification, etc.

If a general manager won't go (to get educated on MRP II), then the company shouldn't go . . . ahead with implementation. It will probably not succeed. Far better not to attempt it, than to attempt it in the face of such long odds.

2. *Line accountability for education.* Remember the ABCs of

MRP II? The A item, the most important element, is the people. It's people who'll make it work.

Education is fundamental to enabling people to make it work. It's teaching the people how to use the tools, and getting them to believe they can work with the tools as a team.

Since education is so fundamental to success, an education program must be structured so that a specific group of key people can be held accountable for making certain that the people get educated properly. The education process must not be delegated to the training department, the personnel department, a few full-time people on the project team or, worst of all, outsiders. To attempt to do so seriously weakens accountability for effective education, and hence, sharply reduces the odds for success.

In order to make possible ownership and behavior change, the process of change must be managed and led by a key group of people. These people need to have the following characteristics:

- They must be held accountable for the success of the change process, hence, the success of MRP II at the operational level of the business.
- They must know, as a group, how the business is being run today.
- They must have the authority to make changes in how the business is being run.

Who are these people? They're the department heads, the operating managers of the business. Who else could they be? Only these operating managers can legitimately be held accountable for success in their areas, be intimately knowledgeable with how the business is being run today in their departments, and have the authority to make changes.

3. *Total immersion for key people.* These managers, these key people who'll facilitate and manage this process of change, first need to go through the change process themselves. They'll need more help with this, since they're the first group in the company to go through the process. What they need is "total immersion," an *intensive,* in-depth educational experience to equip them to do this. Obviously, it's essential that top management understand this need, and enable it to happen.

4. *Total coverage throughout the company.* The question arises: Who in a typical company needs MRP II education? Answer: Darn near everybody. Education has to be widespread because of the need for behavior change so widely throughout the company.

What's needed is to educate the "critical mass," to achieve a high level of MRP II knowledgeability and enthusiasm throughout the entire organization. When that occurs, the result is not unlike a chemical reaction. MRP II becomes "the way we do it around here—the way we run the business."

The critical mass in most companies means *80%—minimum— of all the people in the company* prior to going on the air with MRP, with the balance being educated shortly thereafter. That's *all* of the people—from the folks in mahogany row to the guys and gals on the plant floor running the equipment and working on the line. It also includes the people in the middle—the managers, the supervisors, the buyers, the sales people, etc. One of my colleagues, Dave Garwood, has an excellent way of focusing on the need for widespread education. He does it graphically in Figure 6-2.

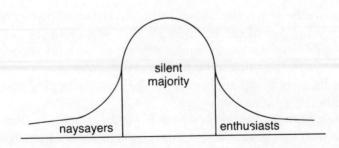

Figure 6-2 Before MRP II Education

There's a small group of people who believe in MRP II, who are enthusiastic, and who want to get going. There's also a small percentage of naysayers, people who don't believe MRP II will work and who are vocally against it. Most folks are in the middle—arms folded, sitting back, not saying much and not expecting much. They're thinking, "Here we go again—another management 'fad' that'll blow over before long."

Here's what needs to happen:

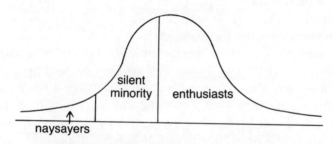

Figure 6-3 After MRP II Education

That's the mission: get a majority of the people enthusiastically on board, reduce the folded-arm set into a minority, and minimize the ranks of the prophets of doom and gloom.

Yes, but (you may be saying to yourself) . . . is it really necessary to educate folks such as group leaders, set-up people, machine operators? You bet it is. Here's one example why:

Harry, an excellent machinist and a hard worker, has been with the company for twelve years. There's been a large queue of work-in-process jobs at Harry's machine during all of those years, except for a time during the early 1980s when business was really bad. Harry got laid off for a while.

Harry's come to associate, perhaps subconsciously, large queues with job security and shrinking queues with reduced business and the possibility of a lay-off.

Question: As the shop floor control portion of MRP II is implemented, what should happen to the queues?

Answer: They should start to decrease dramatically.

Question: When Harry sees the queues dropping, what might he tend to do?

Answer: Slow down.

Question: What will Harry's co-workers tend to do?

Answer: Slow down.

Question: What happens then?

Answer: Output drops, queues don't get smaller, shop floor control doesn't work as well as it should, and so on.

Question: What's the solution?

Answer: Simple. Tell 'em about MRP II. Tell 'em what's coming and why. Tell 'em *how it will affect them and their jobs*.

Telling 'em about it is called education, and it's essential. If you don't tell them what's coming and why, they'll hear about it anyway and will probably assume the worst. Even if you do tell them what and why, they may not believe it all. Our experience, however, has been that most folks in most companies will at least keep an open mind and give it the benefit of the doubt.

The best advice I've ever heard about which people should be educated comes from Walter Goddard, who succeeded Ollie as the head of the Oliver Wight Companies. Walt says, "The question is not 'who to include' in the education process. Rather, it's 'who to *exclude*.' " Right on! Companies should start with the assumption that they'll involve everyone, and then ask themselves who to leave out. One might say, "Well, we really don't need to educate the guy who cuts the grass and shovels the snow. And I guess we could exclude the gals who answer the phones. But do we really want to do that? That could be interpreted that we don't feel these people are important, but that's not true. Everyone who works here is important."

Total coverage means mandatory. Education for MRP II can be optional under only one condition—*if success with MRP II is considered as optional*. On the other hand, if the company's committed to making it work, then it can't be left up to individuals to decide whether or not they'll get educated on MRP II. Education is a process with the objectives of behavior change, teamwork, ownership. The process can't succeed with spotty, sporadic, random participation.

5. *Continuing reinforcement.* Ollie Wight said it well: "Grease gun education doesn't work." He was referring to the "one-shot, quick-hit" type of educational approaches which have been tried so often without lasting results. Retention is poor; it's difficult to get down to the details of how MRP II will work within the company; ownership and, hence, behavior change is very difficult to come by in this environment. What's needed is a program that occurs over an extended period of time. People can learn some things about MRP II, go back and do their jobs, think about what they've learned, let it sink in, evaluate it in the light of how they do their jobs, formulate questions, and then *ask those questions* at the next session.

Repetition is important. When my kids were in grade school, in addition to readin' and 'rithmetic, they also took 'ritin'. Writing in this context means grammar, spelling, punctuation, composition. When they got to high school, they took freshman English which dealt with grammar, spelling, etc. Upon arriving at college, believe it or not, one of the first courses they took was English 101: Grammar and Composition. They took the same subject matter over and over again. Why? Because the ability to speak and write well is so *important.* MRP II is very important; people will need to change the way they do their jobs and run the business. Before that can happen, they'll need to "acquire ownership" of it. To do that, in most cases, means that they'll have to learn about it more than once. Reinforcement facilitates ownership; ownership leads directly to behavior change.

In this process of facilitating behavior change, two-way communications are essential. Putting two hundred people in a hall and talking at them about MRP II may constitute exposure, but not education. The essence of MRP II education is dialogue— where people can discuss, ask questions, and get answers, focus on issues, get specific. It must be involving ("This stuff is interesting") and reassuring ("I'm beginning to see how we can really make this work for us").

People asking questions means people getting believable answers, and this leads us to the next criterion.

6. *Instructor credibility.* Education for MRP II comes in two formats—outside and inside. Both are necessary. It's essential that some key people go to live outside classes, to start to become the company's "experts" on MRP II. It's essential that the instructors of these classes already be "experts," that they've been deeply involved in successful implementations, that they can speak from first-hand experience. If not, credibility will suffer and behavior change for their key people may never get started.

Since it's obviously not practical to send everyone to outside classes, education in-plant is also necessary. The instructors of these classes must not only be knowledgeable on MRP II; they must be "experts" on the company—its products, its processes, its people, its customers, its vendors, etc. If not, credibility will suffer and behavior change for the critical mass may never happen.

7. *Peer confirmation.* It's likely that a given president in a given company feels that he has no peer within that company. Not only is no one on an equal footing, perhaps he feels that no one really understands the problems, the challenges, the requirements of the job.

Interestingly, the vice president of marketing (or finance, or engineering, or whatever) may feel exactly the same way—that they have no peer within the company when it comes to their job. And so might the purchasing manager feel that way, and the assembly superintendent, and others.

Peer confirmation is essential to build confidence in success, so that the process of acquiring ownership can take place. The education program must support this, with a mix of both outside and inside sessions. Outside classes enable key people in similar jobs at different companies to talk, share experiences, compare notes and use each other as a sounding board.

Inside classes are best grouped departmentally. When a number of people in similar jobs are in the same class, peer confirmation, hence, ownership, hence, behavior change are facilitated. The foremen can talk to the other foremen, hear them ask questions, hear the answers coming back from their boss (who's been to one or more outside classes). This process is reassuring. It lowers the level of uncertainty and anxiety; it raises the level of confidence in success; it builds ownership. It enables people to see the need to change the way they do their jobs.

Let's go back to outside classes for a moment. They make another major contribution, in that they get at the "Uniqueness Syndrome." One of the things heard from time to time is: "We're unique. We're different. MRP II won't work for us." Almost invariably, this comes from people who've not yet received proper MRP II education.

One of the key missions of outside education is to help people work through the uniqueness syndrome, to begin to see MRP II as a generalized set of tools which has virtually universal application potential. This is best done, by far, at a live outside class with people from a variety of different companies, with different products, in different types of industries.

8. *Enthusiasm.* Remember the Catch-22 of MRP II? It's a lot of work; we have to do it ourselves; it's not the number one priority. Widespread enthusiasm is one of the key elements needed to break through the Catch-22.

Enthusiasm comes about when people begin mentally to match up their problems (late shipments, massive expediting, excessive overtime, parts shortages, finger pointing, funny numbers, and on and on) with MRP II as the solution. The kind of enthusiasm we're talking about here doesn't necessarily mean the flag-waving, rah-rah variety. More important is a solid conviction that might go like this:

"MRP II makes sense. It's valid for our business. If we do it right, we can solve many of the problems which have been nagging us for years. We as a company can become more competitive, more secure, more prosperous—and we can have more fun in the process."

Most successful MRP II implementations happen without hiring lots of extra people. It's the people already on board who fix the inventory records, the bills, the routings; do the education; solve the problems and knock down the road blocks—and all the while

they're making shipments and running the business as well or
better than before. Here's Ollie again: "Those who've been through
a Class A MRP II installation repeatedly use the phrase 'a sense
of mission.' To those who haven't, that may sound like an over-
statement. It isn't."

The Change Process

Thus far we've looked at the *objectives* of the MRP II education
program, the most important by far being behavior change, and
also the necessary *criteria* for such a program. Now let's look at
the *process* itself, a process which will meet the above criteria
and enable behavior change to happen. This process has to bring
people to see the need and benefits from running the business
differently and, hence, of the need and benefits from doing their
jobs differently.

There are two major aspects of this change process. First, *create
the team of experts,* and secondly, *reach the critical mass* of people
within the company.

CREATE THE TEAM OF EXPERTS

The future team of experts has already been identified—the department heads, the operating managers of the business. Let's
now take a look at how it happens—at how the operating management group within a company becomes a team of experts to
facilitate and manage the change process.

Very simply, this is done by having these people themselves go
through the process of change. The following steps are involved:

1. *Outside classes.* It's essential for this future team of experts
to get away fom the plant or office, for an in-depth educational
experience on MRP II. (See Criterion #3—Total immersion for
key people.)

Such a class should not be "company-specific" or even "industry-
specific." It's important that a variety of companies and industries

be represented in the class. Then the future teams of experts are much better able to work through the issue of uniqueness. They can learn that "We're not unique; we're not different; MRP II will work for us." Similarly, in such a class, there should be a variety of job functions represented—production managers, engineers, marketeers, accountants, materials people, etc. (See Criterion #7—Peer confirmation.)

Of course, these outside classes must be taught by MRP II professionals, people who have a solid track record of participating in successful, Class A implementations of MRP II. These instructors need to be able to communicate not only the principles, techniques and mechanics of MRP II, they must also be able to speak to *results*, the benefits which companies have realized from MRP II.

Here's some good news. Virtually all of the members of the future team of experts have already been to outside classes, as a part of First-Cut Education (see Chapter 4). A number of them will need to attend one or several specialty classes, and perhaps a few haven't been to class at all yet, and hence, will need to go. (Similarly, most of the top management group has already received most of their outside education, again via the First-Cut process.)

2. *A Series of Business Meetings.* Next on the agenda for these folks is to go through a series of business meetings. The objectives here are to continue and enhance the change process begun in the outside classes, and to equip these operating managers with the tools to reach the critical mass.

Doing this properly requires a substantial amount of time, in the neighborhood of eighty hours spread over several months. Not nearly as much time would be required here if the only objective were fact transfer. However, since the main objective is behavior change, be prepared for a substantial commitment of time. (See Criteria #3—Total immersion for key people, and #5—Continuing reinforcement.)

Since we refer to these sessions as a series of business meetings, the question arises: "Does any education take place at these meetings?" Yes indeed. Education is essential, as a means to the end of making behavior change happen.

It needs to occur at three levels:

- principles, concepts and techniques
- application
- training

Principles, concepts and techniques relate to the defined body of knowledge that we call Manufacturing Resource Planning—the various functions, how they tie together, the need for feedback, the details of how planned orders are created, how the available-to-promise quantity is calculated, the mechanics of the dispatch list, etc. The next level involves the *application* of those principles, concepts and techniques into the individual company. It gets at the details of "how we're going to make this set of tools work for us."

Training is not synonymous with education. Rather, it's a subset of education . . . Training is heavily software dependent. It involves things like how to interpret the master schedule report, what keys to hit on the CRT to release a production order, how to record an inventory transaction, etc. See Figure 6-4.

Figure 6-4 MRP II Training and Education

	Training	*Education*
Focus:	Details and specific aspects of the software	Principles, concepts and techniques, and their application to the business
Emphasis:	Technical	Managerial
Will determine:	How you operate the system	How well you manage the business

A key point: don't train before you educate. People need to know "what" and "why" before they're taught "how." Education should occur either prior to, or simultaneously with, training.

The series of business meetings should function at all three levels. However, it may not be possible to do all of the training at this point. This would be so if new software were required but not yet selected. In such a case, the software aspects of training would have to be done later, after the new software package had been chosen. In any case, don't delay education waiting for all of the training materials to be available. See Figure 6-5 for an outline of a typical session.

Figure 6-5 Typical MRP II Session

Activity	Purpose	Ratio of Total Time Spent
Presentation of Educational Materials	Fact Transfer	$1/3$
Discussion	Behavior Change	$2/3$

The agenda for these business meetings needs to be provided by the educational materials themselves. A variety of media are possible candidates. Today, however, companies serious about MRP II almost unvariably use professionally developed video taped courses, supplemented by printed material.

Some of the educational material presented to the future (and rapidly developing) team of experts will contain specific topics which are new to them. However, much of it should be material to which they've already been exposed. These are key people, and they'll need to hear a number of things more than once. (See Criterion #5—Continuing reinforcement.)

The heart of these business meetings is that approximately two-thirds of the time is devoted to discussion. This is where the key people focus on *application,* on how the tools of MRP II will be used within the company to run the business. It's in these business meetings where, for example, the production manager might say:

"OK, I understand about shop floor control and dispatch lists." (Author's note: he understands the principles, concepts and techniques.) "But how are we going to make it work back in Department 15? Man, that's a whole different world back there."

The production manager in this case, and in a larger sense the

company, needs an answer. How are we going to schedule Department 15 using the tools contained within MRP II? Perhaps
the answer can be obtained right in the same session, following
some discussion. Perhaps it needs some research, and the answer
might not be forthcoming until the following week. Perhaps it's
a very sticky issue. Input from the consultant may be sought,
either at his next visit or via the telephone. A spin-off task force
may be required, perhaps with the production manager as the
leader. This is the right way to "design the system."

It's what my colleague, Bill Hartman, calls "bulletproofing"
MRP II. People need to have opportunities to "take potshots"
at MRP II, to try to shoot holes in it. That's what the production
manager just did. Giving people answers which make sense helps
to bulletproof MRP II. Making necessary changes to how the
system will be used is further bulletproofing. Bulletproofing isn't
instantaneous; it's not like turning on a light bulb. It's a gradual
process, the result of responding to people's questions and being
sensitive to their concerns.

Bulletproofing doesn't happen when someone doesn't get valid
answers to questions, or when *essential* changes are not recognized. In that case, MRP II has just had a hole shot in it. Holes
in MRP II mean that ownership won't take place, and therefore,
behavior change won't happen.

Most people need to:

- understand it,
- think about it,
- talk to each other about it,
- ask questions about it and get answers,
- hear their peers ask questions about it and get answers,
- see how it will help them and help the company,

before they'll willingly and enthusiastically proceed to change the
way they do their jobs.

A word about enthusiasm. (See Criterion #8.) During this
series of business meetings, enthusiasm should noticeably start to
build. Enthusiasm is the visual signal that the change process is

happening. If that signal isn't forthcoming, then the change process is probably not happening. Stop right there. Fix what's not being done properly before moving forward.

Who's the best person to run these business meetings for the team of experts? Probably the project leader. He has more time to devote to getting ready to lead each meeting, and subsequently, getting answers to questions. Some companies have varied this approach somewhat, with fine results. What they've done is to have the project leader initially run the meetings, lead the discussions, etc. However, after several weeks (of five meetings per week), as enthusiasm noticeably starts to build, the meetings can start to be run by others in the group. This gets the managers accustomed to running these kinds of meetings before they start leading the sessions for their own departments.

For a recap of what we've covered for the team of experts, see Figure 6-6.

Figure 6-6 Creating the Team of Experts

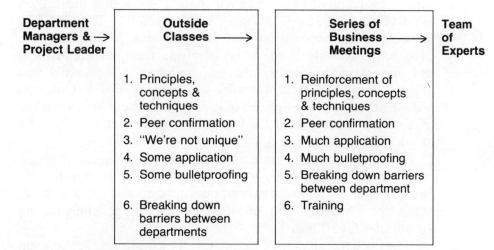

Department Managers & → Project Leader	Outside Classes ⟶	Series of Business ⟶ Meetings	Team of Experts
	1. Principles, concepts & techniques	1. Reinforcement of principles, concepts & techniques	
	2. Peer confirmation	2. Peer confirmation	
	3. "We're not unique"	3. Much application	
	4. Some application	4. Much bulletproofing	
	5. Some bulletproofing	5. Breaking down barriers between department	
	6. Breaking down barriers between departments	6. Training	

REACH THE CRITICAL MASS

Once the team of experts is created, the next step is for them to reach the *critical mass*. This is that majority of people within the company who are knowledgeable and enthusiastic about MRP II, and who see the need and benefits from changing the way they do their jobs.

How is this accomplished? Very simply, by a *series of business meetings*. These are meetings conducted by the members of the team of experts (see Criterion #6—Instructor credibility) for all of the people within their respective departments (see Criteria #2—Line accountability for education and #4—Total coverage throughout the company). Figure 6-7 depicts this process graphically.

All of the other people in the company? Yes. Including top management? Definitely. Even though they went to an outside class on MRP II? Yes indeed, for a number of reasons, but primarily because for MRP II to succeed, they will need to *change the way they do their job* in many respects. They will need to manage the business differently than they have in the past. Attending a two-day outside class on MRP II is rarely sufficient to make possible that kind of behavior change on a permanent basis.

Top management people, like everyone else, need repetition and reinforcement. They need to hear some things more than once (Criterion #5—Continuing reinforcement). They need to get deeper into application than they were able to in the outside classes, particularly in the areas of production planning, rough-cut capacity planning and master scheduling. It's essential that they see how these tools will work within the company (Criterion #8—Enthusiasm). They need to lead by example (Criterion #1—Active top management leadership and participation in the education process).

This series of business meetings, for the top management group and others, is very similar to those for the team of experts. The same format is employed (about one-third education, two-thirds discussion); and the duration of these meetings generally should be about 1½ to 2 hours.

A key difference is with frequency. The meetings for the team of experts are normally held every day, because there's urgency to get these folks "up to speed" so they can begin to spread the word. An accelerated schedule like this isn't necessary or desirable for the rest of the people. It's better for them to meet about once per week, learn some new things, discuss them with their

Figure 6-7 Creating the Critical Mass

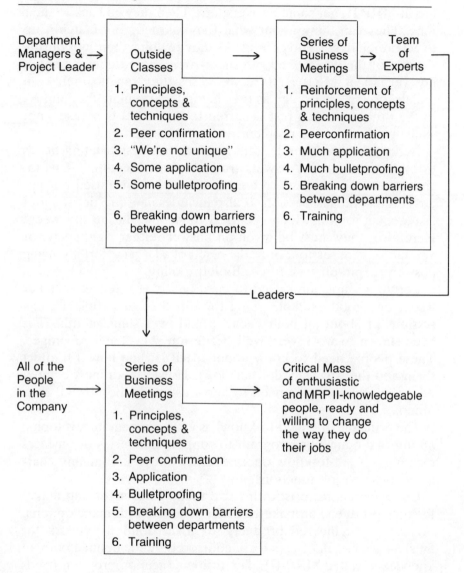

co-workers (Criterion #7—Peer confirmation), shoot some bullets at MRP II, get some answers, etc. Then they go back to their jobs. They can think about what they learned, and match it up to what they're currently doing. As they're doing their jobs during the rest of the week, they can shoot some more bullets (mental, not verbal) at MRP II. In some cases they can do their own bulletproofing, internally, as they mentally formulate the solution to the problem which just occurred to them. In other cases, not so. They think of the problem, but not the solution.

Hence, the first agenda item for each business meeting needs to be "Questions & Answers from the Last Meeting." This includes not only answers to questions which were raised but unanswered at the last session. It also includes *new* questions, about last week's topics, which occurred to people during the week. Here also, they must be given an answer, either right away, or at a subsequent session, or as the result of a larger effort involving possibly a spin-off task force. Bulletproofing.

Certain groups don't need to meet nearly as often as once per week, one good example being the direct labor people. A few sessions of about an hour each, spread over some months, has been shown to work very well (Criterion #4—Total coverage). These people need to know about MRP II, and how it'll affect them and the way they do their jobs. However, in most companies, they simply don't need to know as much about MRP II as others.

The principle of "need-to-know" is a key element in developing an internal education program to support this series of business meetings. Need-to-know operates at two levels: company characteristics and job functions.

Company characteristics involve such things as having make-to-stock products, or make-to-order products with many options, or custom engineered products, or a distribution network for finished goods (all of which are addressed by the defined body of knowledge called MRP II). The inside education program needs to be sensitive to these characteristics. There are few things worse than forcing people to learn a solution to a problem they don't have. What *is* worse is not giving them the solution to a problem they do have.

The second element of need-to-know reflects the different functions within a company, which calls for different "depths" of education and discussion. This gets us back to reinforcement—the concept that people need to hear the important things more than once. Well, what's very important to people in one department may be less so to another.

For example, the vice president of marketing does not need to know a great deal about the mechanics of generating the shop dispatch list. He does need to know that this tool exists, that it's valid, and that it's derived via a rack-and-pinion relationship from material requirements planning, the master schedule, and the production plan.

The buyers need to know more about the shop dispatch list than the VP of marketing. This is because they're buying material to support the shop schedules. They'll need more input and more discussion on this topic. (Conversely, the VP of marketing and other VPs and the general manager will need to know more about production planning than the buyers. Production planning is their responsibility; it's "their part of the ship.")

The foreman and dispatchers need to know all about the shop dispatch list. It's their tool; they'll be living with it every day. They'll need more education, more discussion, more bulletproofing on this topic than the buyers or just about anyone else.

One last point regarding the principle of need-to-know—the educational materials must lend themselves to need-to-know. They must be comprehensive and detailed. They should be able to be tailored to reflect company characteristics and to support the differing levels of depth required by the various departments and job functions.

How does one know if it's working, this process of change? What's the test to apply as the sessions proceed? Here also, the test is *enthusiasm* (see Criterion #8). If enthusiasm, teamwork, a sense of mission and a sense of ownership are not visibly increasing during this process, then stop the process and fix it. Ask "What's missing? What's not being done properly? Which of the eight criteria are being violated? Is bulletproofing working, or are people *not* getting answers?" (That means holes in MRP II, and not many people want to get on board a leaky boat.)

AN ALTERNATIVE APPROACH

Here's an appealing approach to education for MRP II. I call it "Mohammed to the Mountain."

> "Let's not spend all that money on air fare and lodging to send our people away to class. Let's get the 'experts' to bring the class to us, here in the plant or maybe at the Holiday Inn down the street."

Not a bad idea, right? Wrong. It *is* a bad idea, for a number of reasons.

1. *Peer confirmation* can be literally impossible in this environment. The reason is obvious: there are no peers in the class for many of the people (president, VP of engineering, purchasing manager, assembly superintendent, etc.).

2. *The uniqueness syndrome* is very difficult to knock down in an in-plant class taught by outside instructors. By definition everyone in the room is from the same company (except for the "outside experts" who know little or nothing about the company's products, processes and people). What often happens is that the session degenerates into a discussion of making widgets, how difficult widget-making is, why widget-making is unlike other kinds of manufacturing, and on and on. The "outside experts" are at a severe disadvantage. They don't really know the business. They can quickly lose credibility. A certain amount of fact transfer may occur, but the odds for significant behavior change become very poor.

3. *Dialogue* can become constrained. In most in-plant classes, there are many different organizational levels present. The president may be there, plus some of the vice presidents and directors, many of the managers, some supervisors, etc. The more junior people (organizationally) may be reluctant to ask questions, because they don't want to appear foolish in the eyes of their bosses. But that's not all. Some of the more *senior* people in the room may be reluctant to ask questions, because they don't want to appear foolish in the eyes of . . . their subordinates.

4. *Hidden Agendas* are almost always present. In the world of the informal system, with its frequent finger-pointing, deep antagonisms sometimes develop. Often people look upon in-plant classes as an opportunity to, for example, "Nail Charlie to the wall. I've been trying to tell that s. o. b. for years that he's causing big problems." Often the instructor is requested to participate in such a process by introducing a given topic or covering certain material in a certain manner.

I, along with many of my colleagues, used to conduct in-plant classes. To our credit, we don't do them any more, even though they can be very lucrative. We learned (trial and error once again) that they fail the test of generating solid and lasting results. Behavior change rarely results. Some fact transfer may take place, but usually not much else.

A Mini Case Study

Company T (the name has been disguised to protect the successful) sent about a dozen of its senior executives to an outside top management class on MRP II.

The CEO's response after attending was less than completely enthusiastic. He was not anti-MRP II, but rather was lukewarm. This caused great concern to Sam, the project leader, who said the following to your friendly author.

SAM: "Tom, I'm really concerned about our CEO. He's very neutral toward MRP II. With that, I don't think we can succeed."

FRIENDLY AUTHOR (FA): "What do you plan to do about it?"

SAM: "We're going to start the inside education for top management next month. If that doesn't turn our CEO around, I'm going to recommend that we pull the plug on the entire project."

FA: "Sam, you're right. I'll back you up 100%."

Company T started the series of MRP II business meetings for its top management, with the CEO in attendance. After a half dozen or so sessions, the lukewarm CEO got the fire lit. He did, among other things, the following:

1. Sent a memo to each one of his nine division managers, directing them to send him each week a report listing any unauthorized absences from the internal MRP II education sessions.

2. He would then send a personal letter to each person so identified. He would express his concern over their unauthorized absence, ask them to attend the make-up session as soon as possible, and to do everything they could to avoid missing future sessions.

Needless to say, people receiving such a letter would be very unlikely to miss future sessions. So would their fellow foremen and buyers and sales people and schedulers, because the word quickly got around.

Within a few years, all nine of Company T's divisions were operating at a Class A level. The key to their success—education. They did it right.

- They educated virtually everyone in the company.
- They educated from top to bottom, from the CEO to the machine operators.
- They educated both outside and inside. (Note: it wasn't until *inside* education that the CEO really got on board. Why? I'm not sure. One cause could be the need for reinforcement, the need to hear some things more than once. Or perhaps it was getting down to specifics. Some folks really can't get the fire lit until they can see in specific terms how MRP II's going to be used in the company.)
- Education became mandatory, thanks to the CEO and the repeated education he received. Success also became mandatory.

And succeed they did.

IMPLEMENTER'S CHECKLIST

Function: EDUCATION

Task	Complete	
	Yes	No
1. All members of executive steering committee, including general manager, to outside MRP II class.	____	____
2. All members of project team to outside MRP II class.	____	____
3. Series of business meetings conducted for operating managers, completing the total immersion process and resulting in the "team of experts."	____	____
4. Series of business meetings conducted by the team of experts for all persons within the company, including the general manager and staff.	____	____
5. Enthusiasm, teamwork and a sense of ownership becoming visible throughout the company.	____	____

Chapter 7

Data and Policies

It's essential to build a solid foundation of highly accurate numbers *before* master production scheduling and material requirements planning "go on the air." Accurate numbers *before* MPS and MRP, not during or after.

Also during this period, it's necessary to develop certain policies that will set the ground rules and give direction to people in their day-to-day activities.

Data

An enormous amount of data is necessary to operate MRP II. Some of it needs to be highly accurate; some doesn't.

Data for MRP II can be divided into two general categories: *forgiving* and *unforgiving*. Forgiving data can be less precise; it doesn't need to be accurate "to four decimal places." Unforgiving data is just that—unforgiving. It has little margin for error. If it's not highly accurate, it can harm MRP II, perhaps fatally, quickly and without mercy.

Examples of unforgiving data include: inventory balances, scheduled receipts, allocations, bills of material, and routings (excluding standards). Forgiving data includes things like lead times, order quantities, safety stocks, standards, demonstrated capacities, forecasts, etc.

The typical company will need to spend far more of its collective time, effort, blood-sweat-and-tears, and money to get the unforgiving data accurate. The forgiving data shouldn't be neglected, but kept in its proper perspective.

UNFORGIVING DATA

Inventory balances

The inventory balances (on-hand balances) in the computer must be 95% accurate, at a minimum. Do not attempt to implement master scheduling and MRP without at least this level of accuracy. See Figure 7-1.

The inventory balance numbers are vitally important because they represent the "starting number" for material requirements planning. If the balance for an item is not accurate, the planning for it will probably also be incorrect. If the planning is incorrect for a given item, such as a subassembly, then the erroneous planned orders will be exploded into incorrect gross requirements for all of that subassembly's components. Hence, the planning will probably be incorrect for those items also. The result: large amounts of incorrect recommendations coming out of MRP, a loss of confidence by the users, a return to using the hot list, and an unsuccessful implementation of MRP II.

What specifically does 95% accuracy mean? *Of all the on-hand balance numbers inside the computer, 95% should match what is physically on the shelf in the stockroom.*

"But that's impossible!" people say. "What about all the nuts and bolts and shims and washers and screws and so forth? These are tiny little parts, they're inexpensive, and we usually have thousands of any given item in stock. There's no way to get the computer records to match what's actually out there."

Enter the concept of *counting tolerance*. Items such as fasteners are normally not hand-counted but scale-counted. (The stock is weighed, and then "translated" into pieces by a conversion factor.) If, for example, the scale is accurate to plus or minus 2%, and/or the parts vary a bit in weight, then it obviously isn't practical to insist on an exact match of the count to the book record. In cases where items are weigh-counted (or "volume-counted," such as liquids in a tank), companies assign a counting tolerance to the item. In the example above, the counting tolerance might be plus or minus 3%. Any physical count within plus or minus

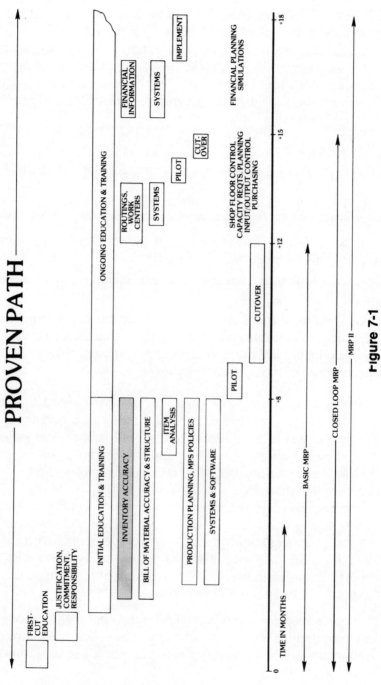

PROVEN PATH

FIRST-CUT EDUCATION

JUSTIFICATION, COMMITMENT, RESPONSIBILITY

INITIAL EDUCATION & TRAINING

ONGOING EDUCATION & TRAINING

INVENTORY ACCURACY

BILL OF MATERIAL ACCURACY & STRUCTURE

ITEM ANALYSIS

PRODUCTION PLANNING, MPS POLICIES

SYSTEMS & SOFTWARE

PILOT

CUTOVER

ROUTINGS, WORK CENTERS

SYSTEMS

PILOT

CUT-OVER

FINANCIAL INFORMATION

SYSTEMS

IMPLEMENT

SHOP FLOOR CONTROL
CAPACITY REQTS. PLANNING
INPUT/OUTPUT CONTROL
PURCHASING

FINANCIAL PLANNING
SIMULATIONS

TIME IN MONTHS

0   +8   +12   +15   +18

BASIC MRP

CLOSED LOOP MRP

MRP II

Figure 7-1

3% of the computer record would be considered a "hit," and the computer record would be accepted as correct.

Given this consideration, let's expand the earlier statement about accuracy: 95% of all the on-hand balance numbers inside the computer should match what is physically on the shelf inside the stockroom, *within the counting tolerance.* Don't leave home (i.e., go on the air) without it.

There are a few more things to consider about counting tolerances. The method of handling and counting an item is only one criterion for using counting tolerances. Others include:

1. The *value* of an item. Inexpensive items will tend to have higher tolerances than the expensive ones.

2. The frequency and volume of *usage.* Items used more frequently will be more subject to error.

3. The *lead time.* Shorter lead times can mean higher tolerances.

4. The *criticality* of an item. More critical items require lower tolerances or possible zero tolerance. For example, items at higher levels in the bill are more likely to be "shipment stoppers"; therefore, they may have lower tolerances.

The cost of control obviously should not exceed the cost of inaccuracies. The bottom line is the validity of the material plan. The range of tolerances employed should reflect their impact on the company's ability to produce and ship on time. Our experience shows Class A users use tolerances ranging from 0 to 5%, with none greater than 5%.

The question that remains is how a company achieves the necessary degree of inventory accuracy. The answer involves some very basic management principles. Provide people with the right tools to do the job, teach the people how to use the tools (called education and training, right?), and then hold them accountable for results. Let's take a closer look.

1. A *"zero defects" attitude.* This is the "people" part of getting and maintaining inventory accuracy. The folks in the stockroom need to understand inventory record accuracy is very important, and therefore, *they* are important. The points the company must make go like this:

a. MRP II is very important for our future. It will make the company more prosperous, and our jobs more secure.

b. Material requirements planning is an essential part of making MRP II work.

c. Inventory accuracy is an essential part of making material requirements planning work.

d. The people who are responsible for inventory accuracy are important. How well they do their jobs makes a big difference.

2. *Limited access.* This is the "hardware" part of getting accuracy. In most cases, limited access means having the area physically secured—fenced and locked. Psychological restrictions can be effective, but should be used only where necessary.

The stockrooms need to be secured, but not primarily to keep people out, although that's the effect. The primary reason to secure the stockrooms is to *keep accountability in.* In order to hold the stockroom foreman accountable for inventory accuracy, the company must give him the necessary tools. One of these is the ability to control who goes in and out of the stockroom. That means limiting access exclusively to those who need to be there. Then, the stockroom foreman can be the "captain of the ship" and may be legitimately held accountable for results.

Let me add a word of caution about locking up the stockroom. It can be a very emotional issue. In the world of the informal system, many manufacturing people (foremen, general foremen, superintendents) spend a lot of time in the stockroom. They do this not because they think the stockroom is a great place to be. They're in the stockroom trying to get *parts,* to make the *product,* so they can *ship* it. It's called expediting, and they do it in self-defense.

If, one morning, these people come to work to find the stockrooms fenced and locked, the results can be devastating. They've just lost the only means by which they've been able to do their jobs.

Before locking up the stockrooms, do three things:

a. Tell the people in advance the stockrooms are going to be locked. Don't let it come as a surprise.

b. Tell them *why*. It's not theft. It's accountability. It's being done to get the records accurate, so that MRP can work.

c. Tell them Priority #1 is service—service to the production floor, service to the repair department, service to shipping, service to the customer, etc.

In a company implementing MRP II, Priority #1 is to run the business; Priority #2 is implementation. In the stockroom, Priority #1 is service and Priority #2 is getting the inventory records accurate.

Make certain that everyone, both in and out of the stockrooms, knows these things *in advance*.

3. *A good transaction system.* This is the "software" part of the process. The system for recording inventory transactions and updating stock balances should be simple, and should represent reality.

"Simple" implies easy to understand and easy to use. It means only a few transaction types. Some software packages contain many unnecessary transaction types. After all, what can happen to inventory? It goes into stock, and out of it. That's two transaction types. It can go in or out on a planned or unplanned basis. That's four. Add one for a stock-to-stock transfer and perhaps several others for inventory adjustments and miscellaneous activities. There are still probably less than ten different transaction types that are really needed. Just because the software package has thirty-two different types of inventory transactions doesn't mean the company needs to use them all in order to get its money's worth. Using too many unnecessary transaction types makes the system unduly complicated, which makes it harder to operate, which makes it that much more difficult to get and keep the records accurate. Who needs this? Remember, *stockroom people* will be using these tools, not PhDs in computer science. Keep it simple. Less is more.

The transaction system should also be a valid representation of reality—how things happen in the real world. For example, on-hand balances should be updated as items move into and out of stock. This means avoiding widespread use of techniques like backflush, pre-deduct, and post-deduct. In these techniques, inventory balances are updated substantially before or after the movement of the material, not coincident with it, and cycle counting can become far more difficult.

Another example of representing reality: inventory by location. Many companies stock items in more than one bin in a given stockroom, and/or in more than one stockroom. Their transaction systems should have the capability to reflect this.

A third example: quick updates of the records. Inventory transaction processing does not have to be done in real time. However, it should be done fairly frequently and soon after the actual events have taken place. No transaction should have to "wait" more than twenty-four hours to be processed.

4. *Cycle counting.* This is the mechanism through which a company gains and maintains inventory record accuracy. It has four main objectives:

a. *To discover the causes of errors*—so that the causes can be eliminated. The saying about the rotten apple in the barrel applies here. Get it out of there before it spoils more apples. Put more emphasis on prevention than cure. When an inventory error is discovered, fix the record. Also, fix the cause of the error. Was the cause of the error inadequate physical security, a software bug, a bad procedure, or perhaps insufficient training of a stock person? Whenever practical, find the cause of the error, and correct it—so that it doesn't happen again.

b. *To measure results.* Cycle counting needs to answer the question, "How are we doing?" It should frequently generate accuracy percentages, so the people know whether the records are sufficiently accurate. In addition, some companies routinely verify the cycle counting accuracy numbers via independent audits by people from the accounting department, often on a monthly basis. In this way they verify that the stockroom's inventory records are as good as the stockroom people say they are.

c. *To correct inaccurate records.* When a cycle count does not match the computer record, the item should be re-counted. If the results are the same, the on-hand balance in the computer must be adjusted.

d. *To eliminate the annual physical inventory.* This becomes practical after the 95% accuracy level has been reached on an item-to-item basis. Although doing away with it is important, it's not primarily because of the expense involved. The problem is that most annual physical inventories make the records *less* accurate, not more. Over the years, their main purpose has been to verify the balance sheet, not to make the records more accurate.

Consider the following scenario in a company implementing MRP II. The stockroom is fenced and locked; the computer hardware and software is operating properly; and the people in the stockroom are educated, trained, motivated and enthusiastic. Inventory record accuracy is 97.3%. (Remember, this is units, not dollars. When the units are 95–99% accurate, the dollars are almost always in the 99% + accuracy range. This is because plus and minus dollar errors cancel each other out; unit errors stand alone.)

It seems to me counterproductive to open the gates to the stockroom one weekend, bring in a bunch of outside auditors, and have them climbing up and down the bins like a bunch of monkeys, writing down numbers and putting them into the computer. What happens to inventory accuracy? It drops. What happens to accountability? There's not much left. What happens to the morale of the people in the stockroom? It's gone—it just flew out the open gates.

Avoid taking annual physical inventories once the records are at least 95% accurate. Most major accounting firms won't insist on them. They will want to do a spot audit of inventory accuracy, based on a statistically valid sample. They'll probably also want to review the cycle counting procedures, to audit the cycle count results, and to verify the procedures for booking adjustments. That's fine. But there should be no need to take any more complete physical inventories, not even "one last one to confirm the records." Having accounting people doing a monthly audit of inventory accuracy (as per paragraph b above) can facilitate this entire process of eliminating the annual physical inventory. This comes about because the accounting folks are involved routinely, and can begin to feel confidence and ownership of the process.

An effective cycle counting system contains certain key characteristics. First of all, it's done *daily*. Counting some parts once per month or once per quarter won't get the job done.

Good cycle counting procedures often contain a *control group*. This is a group of a hundred or so parts which are counted every week. The purpose of the control group gets us back to the first objective of cycle counting—discovering the *causes* of errors. This is far easier to determine with parts counted last week than with those checked last month, last quarter, or last year.

Ease of operation is another requirement of an effective system. It's got to be easy to compare the cycle count to the book record, easy to reconcile discrepancies, and easy to make the adjustment after the error has been confirmed.

Most good cycle counting systems require a *confirming recount*. If the first count is outside the tolerance, that merely indicates the probability of an error. A recount is necessary to confirm the error. With highly accurate records, often it's the count that's wrong, not the record.

Lastly, a good cycle counting system should *generate and report measures of accuracy*. A percentage figure seems to work best—total hits (good counts) divided by total counts. (Exclude from these figures counts for the control group; within a few weeks, the control group should be at or near 100%.) Report these numbers frequently, perhaps once per week, to the key individuals—stockroom people, project team, steering committee, etc. Post them on bulletin boards or signs where other people can see them.

Get count coverage on all items, and 95% minimum accuracy, *before* going live with material requirements planning. In many companies, cycle counting must be accelerated prior to going on the air in order to get that coverage. The company may need to allocate additional resources to make this possible.

Once the stockroom has reached 95% inventory record accuracy, don't stop there. That's merely the *minimum* number for running MRP II. Don't be satisfied with less than 98% accuracy. Our experience has been that companies which spend all the money and do all the things necessary to get to 95% need only dedication and hard work and good management to get in the 98–99% range. Make sure everyone knows that going from 95% to 98% is not merely an accuracy increase of 3%. It really is a 60% reduction in exposure to error, from 5% to 2%. MRP II will operate a good deal better with only 1 or 2% of the records wrong than with 4 or 5%.

There are two other elements involved in inventory status which need to be mentioned: scheduled receipts and allocations. Both elements must be at least 95% accurate prior to turning on MRP.

Scheduled receipts

Scheduled receipts come in two flavors: open shop orders and open purchase orders. They need to be accurate on quantity and *order* due date. Note the emphasis on the word "order." Material requirements planning doesn't need to know the *operational* due dates and job location of shop orders. It does need to know when the order is due to be completed, and how many pieces remain on the order. Don't make the mistake of thinking that shop floor control must be implemented first in order to get the numbers necessary for material requirements planning.

Typically, the company must review all scheduled receipts, both shop orders and purchase orders, to verify quantity and timing. Then, establish good order close-out procedures to keep "residual garbage" from building up in the scheduled receipt files.

In some companies, however, the shop orders can represent a real challenge. Typically, these are companies with high speeds and high volumes. In this kind of environment, it's not unusual for one order to "catch up" with an earlier order for the same item. Scrap reporting can also be a problem. Reported production may be applied against the wrong shop order.

Here's what I call "A Tale of Two Companies" (with apologies to Charles Dickens). In a certain midwestern city, two companies are operating MRP II very successfully. They happen to be located on the same street. That's where the similarity ends. One, Company M, makes machine tools. Company M's products are very complex, and the manufacturing processes are low volume and low speed. This company had to work very hard to get their on-hand balances accurate, because of the enormous number of parts in their stockrooms. They had far less of a challenge to get shop order accuracy, because of the low volumes and low speeds.

Their neighbor down the street, Company E, makes electrical connectors. The product contains far fewer parts than a machine tool. Fewer parts in stock means an easier job in getting accurate on-hand balances. These connectors, however, are made in high volume at high speeds. Company E had to work far harder at getting accurate shop order data. They had to apply proportionately more of their resources to the shop order accuracy, unlike Company M.

The moral of the story: Scratch where it itches. Put the resources where the problems are.

Allocations

Allocations shouldn't be a major problem. If the company has them already, take a "snapshot" of the allocation file, then verify and correct the numbers. (In the worst case, cancel all the unreleased scheduled receipts and allocations and start over.) Also be sure to fix what's caused the errors: bad bills of material, poor stockroom practices, inadequate procedures, etc. If there are no allocations yet, make certain the software is keeping them straight as the company starts to run MRP.

Bills of material

The accuracy target for bills of material is even higher than on inventory balances: 98% minimum, in terms of item number, unit of measure and quantity per parent item. See Figure 7-2. An error in either of these elements will generate requirements incorrectly.

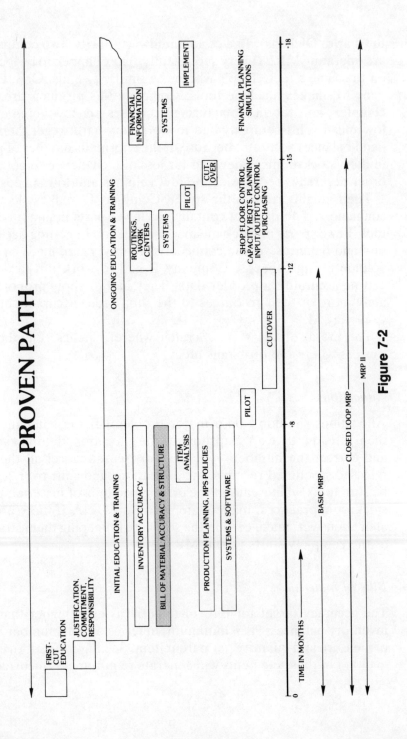

Figure 7-2

Incorrect requirements will be generated into the right components, or correct requirements into the wrong components, or
both.

First of all, what does 98% bill of material accuracy mean? In
other words, how is bill accuracy calculated? Broadly, there are
three approaches: the tight method, the loose method, and the
middle-of-the-road method.

In examining the tight method, assume the bill of material in
Figure 7-3 is in the computer:

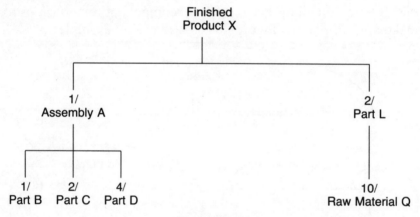

Figure 7-3

Suppose there's only one incorrect relationship here—Assembly
A really requires *five* of Part D, not four. (Or perhaps it's Part
D that's not used at all, but in fact four of a totally different part
is required.) The tight method of calculating bill accuracy would
call the entire bill of material for finished product X a "miss,"
zero accuracy. No more than 2% of all the products could have
misses and still have the bills considered 98% accurate.

Is this practical? Sometimes. We've seen it used by companies
with relatively simple products, usually with no more than fifty
to a hundred components per product.

The flip side is the loose method. This goes after each one-to-
one relationship, in effect each "line" on the printed bill of material. Using the example above, the following results would obtain:

Misses	Hits
D to A	B to A
	C to A
	A to X
	Q to L
	L to X

Accuracy: 5 hits out of 6 relationships, for 83% accuracy. Most companies would find this method too loose, and would probably opt for the middle-of-the-road method. It recognizes hits and misses based on all of the single-level component relationships to make a given parent. Figure 7-4 uses the same example:

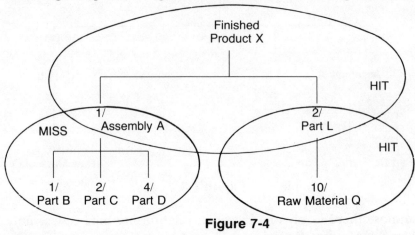

Figure 7-4

Accuracy: 67%. Overall, this is the approach used most frequently. Use this method unless there are strong reasons to the contrary. Once again, the bottom line is the validity of the material plan.

Once the company's decided how to calculate bill of material accuracy, they'll need to determine the measurement approaches to be used, both to acquire accuracy initially, and then to monitor accuracy on an ongoing basis. Here are some options:

1. *Floor audit.* Put some product engineers into the assembly and subassembly areas. Have them compare what's actually being built to the bill of material. They should work closely with not only the foremen, but also with the assemblers. Correct errors as they're discovered.

2. *Office/factory review.* Form a team of engineers, foremen, material planners and perhaps cost people to review the bills jointly, sitting around a conference table. The question to be asked: "Is this the way we build it?" Again, correct errors as they're found.

3. *Product teardown.* Take a finished product apart. Compare the parts and pieces on the table with the computer listing and correct the errors. This can be a good approach, but may be impractical if the product is a jet airliner. Another shortcoming can be the difficulty in recognizing subassemblies.

4. *Unplanned issues/receipts.* When production people go back to the stockroom for more parts, is it because they scrapped some or because they didn't get them in the first place? If the latter is the case, there may be a bill error which caused the picking list to be generated incorrectly.

If parts are returned to stock after the assembly of a product, perhaps they shouldn't have gone out of the shop floor in the first place. Again, the picking list may have been wrong because the bill was wrong. Correct the errors as they're discovered.

This can be a good technique to monitor bill of material accuracy on an ongoing basis.

Certainly, some of these methods are inappropriate for some companies. Select one method, or a combination, and get started as soon as possible. Don't go on the air without 98% accuracy on all bills, because MRP won't work well without very accurate bills.

In addition to being accurate, the bills of material need to be complete, properly structured and integrated.

1. *Completeness.* Bills should include everything involved in making the product—things like raw materials, fasteners, packaging materials, solder and flux, etc. At a minimum, all of the "important stuff" (like raw materials) should be in the bills before turning on MRP. *Many companies would* consider raw materials as "important," standard fasteners less so. The other items should be added as soon as it's practical.

2. *Structure.* Structure has two meanings. First of all, the bills must be properly structured to show stock points, phantoms, etc.

Secondly, companies whose products have many options usually need to structure their bills into a modular format. This is necessary to allow effective forecasting, master scheduling and customer order promising. Caution—estimate the workload closely ahead of time. Typically, it takes many man-months of engineering time to develop modular bills. Don't forget the principle of the three knobs: the work to be done, the calendar time in which it needs to be done, and the resources available to do it.

3. *Integration.* Some companies have a variety of different bill of material files. Engineering has one, but manufacturing has their own. The cost accounting department doesn't like either of those, so they maintain another one to fit their needs.

MRP II represents a company-wide game plan, in units and dollars, so everyone is "singing from the same sheet of music." It's impossible if different departments have different hymnals. After all, the bill of material, along with the routings, represents the network around which MRP II is built. The various bills must be integrated into a single, unified bill which serves the needs of all of the different departments.

Routings

There's good news and bad news about routings. The bad news is that three key elements are unforgiving; they need to be at least 98% accurate. See Figure 7-5. These are operations to be performed, their sequence, and the work centers at which they'll be done. Their accuracy is extremely important because they'll be used by the computer to locate jobs (in shop floor control) and to apply load (in capacity requirements planning). This is where most companies need to apply a fair amount of time and effort, typically by foremen and manufacturing engineers.

The good news is the other key element within the routing, the standards, are forgiving. Extreme accuracy of the standards is not necessary for CRP and shop floor control. This is because they convert a variety of units—pieces, pounds, gallons, feet, etc.— into a common unit of measure: standard hours. Errors, plus and minus, tend to cancel each other out. The law of large numbers has an effect. A good rule of thumb for standards is to try for accuracy of plus or minus 10%. Even if they're generally skewed to the high or low side, the efficiency factor can be used to "translate" the standard hours to clock hours.

Another good rule of thumb: if the standards today are good enough to calculate product costs, payroll and efficiencies, then they'll be accurate enough for MRP II. Companies which already have standards on a "work center by work center" basis typically find that they don't need to spend a great deal of time and effort on them. They'll be checked as part of the routing accuracy effort, and the obviously wrong ones will be fixed. However, most of your time should be spent on the unforgiving elements.

Calculating routing accuracy is fairly straightforward. If, on a given routing, *all* of the operations, sequence numbers, and work centers are correct, that's a hit. Otherwise, it's a miss. The target is to get at least 98 hits out of every 100 routings checked.

Methods for auditing and correcting routings include:

1. *Floor audit.* This usually involves one or more manufacturing engineers following the jobs through the shop, comparing the computer-generated routing to what's actually happening. Here again, they should talk to the operators, the folks who are making the parts. Virtually every element involves an operator to one degree or another. They know what's happening.

2. *Office/factory review.* This normally involves foremen and manufacturing engineering people sitting around a conference table reviewing the computer-generated routings against their knowledge of the shop and any additional documentation available.

3. *Order close-out.* As shop orders are completed and closed out, the actual reporting is compared to the computer-generated routing.

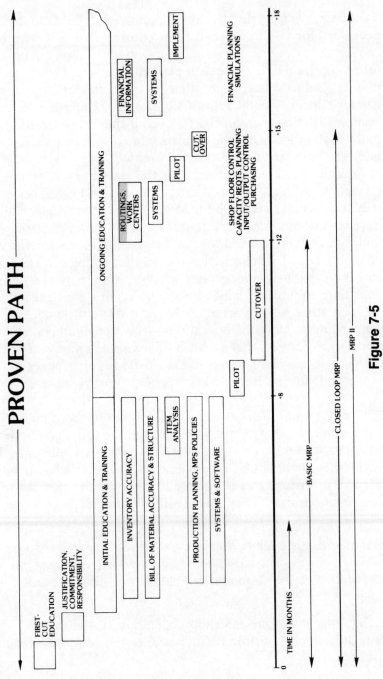

Figure 7-5

Not every method will be practical for every company. Some companies use a combination of several.

Turn again to Darryl Landvater's *Proven Path* bar chart. It calls for going to work on routings and work center data in Month 12, as a part of closing the loop. There's no problem with starting a bit sooner, either. However, please keep in mind that Darryl has established this timetable for companies which *already have routings and standards by work center.* Most companies do.

Companies that don't have routings and standards by work center have a big job ahead of them, and can't afford to wait until Month 12 to begin. They should start just as soon as possible. This part of the project needs to be adequately resourced to do a big job—identify all the work centers, develop routings and standards—without delaying the implementation of the total system. Some companies have had to expand the manufacturing engineering department and/or obtain temporary industrial engineering help from outside the company. This is another case where that cost of a one-month delay number can help a lot with resource allocation/acquisition decisions.

FORGIVING DATA

Virtually all forgiving data is made up of item and work center numbers. In these categories, "four decimal place" accuracy isn't necessary.

Item data

Item data refers to the other numbers necessary for master production scheduling and material requirements planning. See Figure 7-6. Most of it is static and is stored in the computer's *item* file. It includes things like lead times, order quantities, safety stock/time, shrinkage factors, scrap or yield factors (stored in the bill of material), etc.

Getting the item data collected and loaded is a necessary step, but it's normally not a big problem. The people doing it should be the same ones who'll be operating these planning systems: the master scheduler(s), and the material planners. They'll need ed-

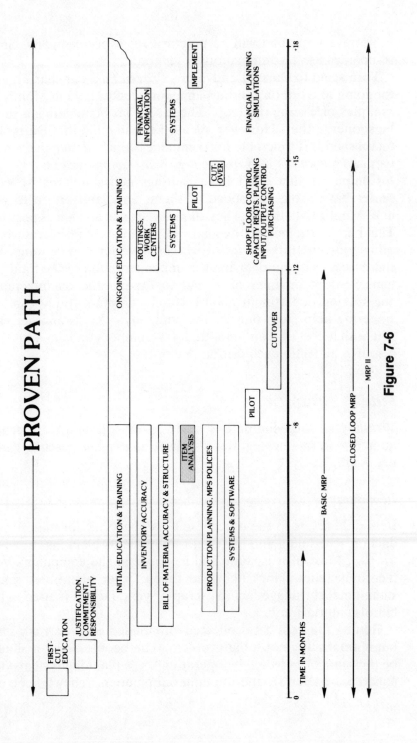

Figure 7-6

ucation, time to do the job, and some policy direction (to be discussed in the next section).

Wherever practical, use the numbers already available. Review them all, make sure they're in the ballpark, and fix the ones that are obviously wrong. If the lead time for an item is obviously too high or too low, change it to a reasonable number; otherwise leave it alone. If the order quantity for a part is out of line, change it; if not, let it be. If an item routinely experiences some scrap loss in production, add in a scrap or shrinkage factor. Otherwise, leave the factor at zero.

The subject of using the numbers already in place leads to a larger issue. When implementing MRP II, *change only what's absolutely necessary to make it work.* Don't make changes for incremental operational improvement, unless they're also necessary for implementation. They'll be plenty of time later, *after* the system is on the air, to fine tune the numbers, and to get better and better.

There are two reasons for this—people and diagnosis:

1. Implementing Manufacturing Resource Planning is a time of great change in a company. For most people, change is difficult. Introducing non-essential changes will make the entire implementation process more difficult than it needs to be.

2. Unnecessary changes also complicate the diagnostic process when something goes wrong. The greater the number of things that were changed, the greater the number of things which could be causing the problem. This makes it correspondingly (perhaps even exponentially) harder to find the problem and fix it.

Work center data

The information involved here includes things like work center identification, demonstrated capacity, efficiency (or productivity) factors, and desired queues. See Figure 7-7.

Review the work center arrangement now being used. Ask whether the machines have been correctly grouped into work centers, and whether the operator skill groups have been established properly. A key factor here—how does each foreman view

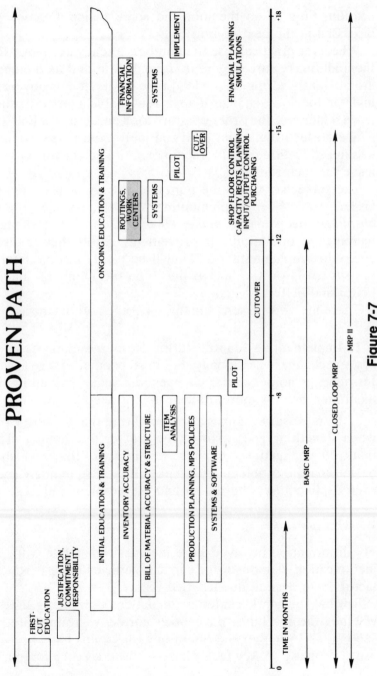

PROVEN PATH

Figure 7-7

the equipment and people in his department, in terms of elements to be scheduled and loaded?

Make whatever changes are necessary. The goal is to enable CRP, input/output and shop dispatching to give the foreman the right information as to workload, priorities and schedule performance.

Realize that changes in work center identification will mean changes to the routings. A good bit of work may be involved. A computer program can often help in revising routings to reflect new work center assignments.

Start to gather statistics for each work center: demonstrated capacity, efficiency (which may already be available) and planned queue. This last element may represent a dramatic change. For most companies, planned queues will be smaller than they were under the informal system. Many companies determine their queues by considering "the range" and "the pain." "Range" refers to the variability of job arrival at the work centers, while "pain" means how much it will hurt if the queue for a particular work center disappears, and it runs out of work.

The key players in these decisions are the foremen and the industrial engineers. Usually, the engineers develop the numbers, while the foremen are more involved with the "qualitative" information—such as grouping equipment for the best work center arrangement, the amount of pain involved if the center runs out of work, etc. Foremen "buy-in" is critical here. Therefore, they, and their bosses, must call the shots. They, and their people, are the ones who'll be accountable for making it work.

Policies

A handful of key policy statements are required for the successful operation of Manufacturing Resource Planning. Four "bedrock" policies are the ones which address production planning, master production scheduling, material planning and engineering change. See Figure 7-8.

The production planning policy should address issues such as

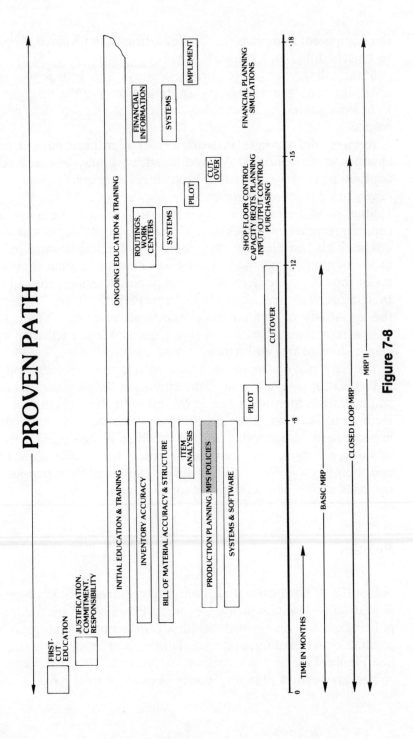

Figure 7-8

who's accountable, who attends the production planning meetings, who develops the data, frequency of the meetings, meeting content, guidelines for making changes to the production plan, product families, etc.

The master production scheduling policy needs to define the roles of the master scheduler and other individuals involved, time fences, who's authorized to make decisions to change the schedule in which time zones, ground rules for promising customer orders, the fact that the MPS must match the production plan, allowable safety stock and/or hedges, feedback requirements from planners, feedback required to sales and marketing, performance measurements, etc.

The material planning policy focuses on guidelines for allowable order quantities, use of safety stock and safety time, where to use scrap and shrinkage factors, ground rules for lead time compression, feedback required from purchasing and plant, feedback to master scheduler, performance measurements, etc.

The engineering change policy should define the various categories of engineering change. Further, for each category, it needs to spell out who's responsible for initiating the change, who establishes effectivity dates, who implements, who monitors. Also included here should be guidelines on new product introduction, communications between engineering and planning, performance measurements, etc.

These are four basic policies which most companies need to operate MRP II effectively, but others may be required for specific situations. Developing these policies is an essential element in the implementation process.

This is another case where both the project team and executive steering committee need to be involved. The project team should:

1. identify the required policies

2. create spin-off task forces to develop them

3. revise/approve the draft policies

4. forward the approved drafts to the executive steering committee.

The steering committee revises/approves the draft policy and the general manager signs it, to go into effect on a given date.

In Chapter 8, I'll examine the subject of MRP II software and systems.

IMPLEMENTERS' CHECKLIST

Function: DATA AND POLICIES

Task	Complete	
	Yes	No
1. Inventory record accuracy, including scheduled receipts and allocations, at 95% or better.	____	____
2. Bill of material accuracy at 98% or better.	____	____
3. Bills of material properly structured, sufficiently complete for MRP II, and integrated into one unified bill for the entire company.	____	____
4. Routings (operations, sequence, work centers) at 98% or better accuracy.	____	____
5. Item data complete and verified for reasonableness.	____	____
6. Work center data complete and verified for reasonableness.	____	____
7. Production planning policy written, approved, and being used to run the business.	____	____
8. Master production schedule policy written, approved, and being used to run the business.	____	____
9. Material planning policy written, approved, and being used to run the business.	____	____
10. Engineering change policy written, approved, and being used to run the business.	____	____

Chapter 8

Software & Systems

Software for MRP II is like a set of golf clubs. Getting in the game requires a reasonably complete set. If Tom Watson went out on the Pro Golfer's Tour with only a four wood and a sand wedge, he probably wouldn't win a lot of money.

On the other hand, Tom *Wallace* might buy the greatest set of clubs in the world and still couldn't break one hundred. I don't know how to play golf.

The moral: software of and by itself cannot make a company a successful MRP II user. However, the lack of a reasonably complete set of software can keep a company from succeeding.

To Buy or Not to Buy

The first software decision a company normally faces is whether to write their own software, or buy an existing package.

There are problems with either approach. First, the bad news about writing one's own software:

1. *It takes too long.* Writing a complete MRP II software package is almost always a multi-year project. As such, it runs counter to all of the reasons for an aggressive implementation schedule. Further, it's prohibitively expensive in light of the cost of a one-month delay. Let's take the case of a company whose one-month delay cost is $100,000. If writing their own software would delay the project by no more than two years, then the resultant delay cost would equal $2,400,000 (24 months × $100,000 per month). That's an expensive piece of software!

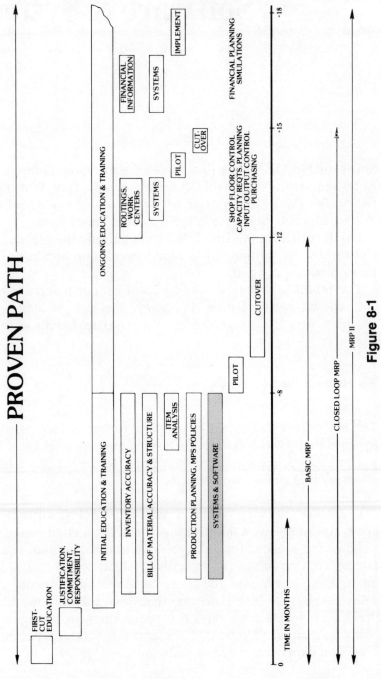

PROVEN PATH

FIRST-CUT EDUCATION

JUSTIFICATION, COMMITMENT, RESPONSIBILITY

INITIAL EDUCATION & TRAINING

ONGOING EDUCATION & TRAINING

INVENTORY ACCURACY

BILL OF MATERIAL ACCURACY & STRUCTURE

ITEM ANALYSIS

PRODUCTION PLANNING, MPS POLICIES

SYSTEMS & SOFTWARE

ROUTINGS, WORK CENTERS

SYSTEMS

FINANCIAL INFORMATION

SYSTEMS

PILOT

PILOT

CUT-OVER

IMPLEMENT

CUTOVER

SHOP FLOOR CONTROL
CAPACITY REQTS. PLANNING
INPUT-OUTPUT CONTROL
PURCHASING

FINANCIAL PLANNING
SIMULATIONS

TIME IN MONTHS

0   ·8   ·12   ·15   ·18

BASIC MRP

CLOSED LOOP MRP

MRP II

Figure 8-1

Errata

The following is a corrected page which should replace page 137 in this book.

2. *It may not work.* During the three or four or more years that it will take to write all the software, there'll be a nagging question which can't be answered with certainty: Will it work? One of the key reasons to buy an existing software package is the ability to see it in operation beforehand. Writing one's own software from scratch may result in software that doesn't work—or doesn't *appear* to work. It could turn out that the software's okay, but the people weren't using it correctly. Hence, good results aren't forthcoming. In that scenario, what is likely to get blamed— the software or the management? Nine times out of ten, the finger would be pointed at the software. Using proven software eliminates the possibility of using software as a scapegoat.

3. *It may be too specific to today's business environment.* Home-grown software for MRP II is usually very specific and very focused on what the company is doing *today.* As such, it may not stand the test of time. Most businesses are dynamic. They change, adapt, grow. One company with which I'm familiar, strictly make-to-stock at the time, implemented MRP II very successfully. They used standard software from an outside source. The software, properly, contained features to support make-to-order master scheduling as well as make-to-stock. The company in question needed the latter but not the former—at the time. Several years later, however, the company developed an entirely new line of products which were make-to-order. Thanks to having standard software, the software tools were already in place to support the new product line. Things might have been far more difficult had they had home-grown software.

Those are some compelling reasons against writing your own software, right? However, don't leap to a decision to buy, not make. Let's examine some of the problems involved with buying a package.

1. *It will be "incomplete."* As this is written, there is no such thing as a totally complete software package for MRP II. Some are woefully incomplete, others less so. Even if a 100% complete package did exist, some modifications or enhancements would be required to "fit it in" to a given company.

1. Allow two days for inspection. (This is a matter of judgment.)

2. Round the standard hours up to the nearest day.

3. Allow X days for queue time.

4. Release work to stockroom one week prior to first operation.

Scheduling with a regular calendar is extremely awkward. For example, if a job was to be completed on August 31 (see Figure A-10) and the last operation—inspection—was scheduled to take two days, the previous operation would have to be completed on August 27, not August 29 (Sunday) or August 28 (Saturday). The scheduler would have to reference the calendar continuously to avoid scheduling work on weekends, holidays, during plant vacation shutdown week, etc. Figure A-11 shows a "shop calendar" where only the working days are numbered. This allows the scheduler to do simple arithmetic like "subtract two days from day 412"; thus the previous operation is to be completed on day 410.

Calendar						
AUGUST						
S	M	T	W	T	F	S
1	2	3	4	5	6	7
8	9	10	11	12	13	14
15	16	17	18	19	20	21
22	23	24	25	26	27	28
29	30	31				

Figure A-10 Calendar

2. *It may be too complicated.* Many of the existing software packages are far more complex than need be. They contain a wide variety of options, features, "bells and whistles," many of which are unnecessary and some of which are counterproductive.

Complexity is bad. For the folks in data processing, it makes the programs difficult to install and maintain. It's a poor choice for the users, too. The users are required to spend a lot of time sorting through all the options, deciding which ones to use. Further, it gives them the opportunity to select improper techniques such as automatic order releasing, automatic rescheduling, finite loading, dynamic lot sizing, etc., which are counterproductive. They inhibit MRP II from working properly.

Last, and probably least in importance, is cost. The more complex software tends to be more expensive. This has led some knowledgeable observers of the MRP II software scene to conclude there is a direct relationship between the cost of software and the time it takes to get it on the air. That relationship is *inverse*. Expensive software tends to be more complex, and complex software is likely to be tougher to install and operate and maintain.

3. *It may be difficult to interface.* Tying new software to existing systems can be an enormous job. I'll expand on this topic later.

4. *It will probably have bugs.* The odds are extremely high that the sun will rise in the east tomorrow morning. Bet on it. The odds are about the same there are bugs in any given software package.

Bugs can be tough to find and fix, and may require help from the software vendor. If that help isn't forthcoming quickly, *the entire MRP II project can be delayed.* Therefore, build some wording into the software contract, as airtight as possible, about bugs, responsibility for fixing them, timing, penalties, etc.

A software vendor's refusal to commit to fixing bugs quickly may be a signal they don't have confidence in their product, or their ability to fix it when it doesn't work, or both. In this case, go somewhere else. They're not the only game in town.

SOME EXAMPLES

Let's take the case of two different companies planning to implement MRP II, which I'll call Company #1 and Company #2. Company #1 has no computer, and no software. Their choice is clear—they need to buy a package. Writing their own would take too long, may not work, etc.

Company #2 attempted to implement MRP several years ago. They purchased a software package which happened to be functionally quite complete. The implementation effort, however, like many others, was flawed. It concentrated largely on installing the software, rather than on the people and data.

Company #2 is a C-minus user. Now they want to re-implement MRP II, and do it right this time. It's very unlikely that they'll need new software because they have virtually all of it already.

Dave Garwood has a good way of communicating this situation graphically by means of a spectrum, or a range of possibilities. Company #1 and Company #2 are at opposite ends of the spectrum. See Figure 8-2.

Figure 8-2

Company #1 —Has None—	Company #2 —Has Almost All—
BUY NEW SOFTWARE	USE WHAT'S THERE

Company #3, a first-time implementer, has had a computer for many years. Over the years, they have developed a number of logistics-related applications on their computer: order entry, inventory transaction processing, shop floor control, bill of material processor, etc. These applications were reasonably well done, but never realized their full potential because the company lacked a formal priority planning system that worked. The work they had done in the areas of master scheduling and material planning wasn't adequate to do away with the informal system. Company #3 is in the middle, somewhere in the uncertain zone. See Figure 8-3.

Company #3 is confronted with a range of alternatives: a) buy all new software, b) buy the missing pieces, c) write the missing

Figure 8-3

	Company #3 —Has Some—	
BUY NEW SOFTWARE	ZONE OF UNCERTAINTY	USE WHAT'S THERE

pieces internally, or d) some combination of b and c. The correct decision will be based on a number of factors: the quality and completeness of what's already in place, the availability of internal resources, the quality of the outside software available or pieces thereof, etc. The final decision should be based on the shortest distance between Company #3's position today and a functionally complete set of software. Which alternative will get them there the fastest; what's the route of least pain?

Selecting Software

Okay, suppose a company has looked at their situation closely, and decided they'll need to buy all or most of their MRP II software. They'll need to select a software package, and that leads us to what I call the "Six P's" of software selection:

1. *Don't be Premature.* Some companies' first exposure to MRP II is through the software salesman who sells them a package. Often, these people regret having made the purchase after they've gone to class and learned about MRP II.

The right way is to learn about MRP II first, and get the software later.

2. *Don't Procrastinate.* This isn't as contradictory as it sounds. Don't make the mistake of trying to find the "perfect" software package, or even the "best" one. That's like searching for the Holy Grail or the Perfect Wave. There is no "best" software package.

The correct approach, after learning about MRP II and deciding to do it, is to get a good workable set of software. An excellent set of tools to help in this process is a series of software evaluations available from Oliver Wight Software Research, Inc. (See Appendix D.) These evaluations are designed to enable companies to learn what they need to know about individual software packages *quickly*. It's important to move through this selection phase with deliberate haste, so the company can get on with implementing MRP II and start getting paybacks.

3. *Don't Pioneer.* As Walt Goddard pointed out in the foreword, pioneers, people who get too far out in front, often get arrows in their backs. This certainly applies to software for MRP II. Why buy untested, unproven software? Beats the hell out of me. Stay away from "brand-new" software.

Insist on seeing the package working in a company operating at a Class A or high B level. (Class A or high B implies all or most of the functions of MRP II are being exercised. Class C companies use the formal system mainly to launch orders.) If the prospective software supplier can't name a Class A or B user of their product, I recommend you don't buy it. Go elsewhere.

However, you may not have much of a choice. Your computer may be one for which no proven software exists. In this case, learn as much as possible about the packages available, and select one that appears simple and easy to modify. Then, plan on having *major problems* with the package; plan to apply *more resources* than normal to making it work; and recognize that the entire MRP II project will probably *take longer and cost more.*

Some companies, when confronted with this problem, make what can be a very intelligent choice. They get a new computer, one that has proven software available.

4. *Minimize Pain.* From a data processing point of view, some of the most difficult parts of an MRP II project are often:

a. installing the software—just getting it to run on the computer.

b. interfacing the software with existing applications that will remain following MRP II implementation (payroll, sales analysis, payables, general ledger, etc.).

c. having to write "throw-away" programs that will be run only once, or for only a short period of time. Often these are "bridges" from the old system to the new. This can sometimes be difficult emotionally for the folks in data processing. It's a bit like building a building that one knows will be torn down three weeks later.

However distasteful it may be, though, some amount of throwaway programming is almost always necessary. Be prepared to do some.

Remember, the more complex the software, the tougher the task will be of installing it. Therefore, all things being equal, choose the simpler package.

In some companies, interfacing can be a massive problem, perhaps the single biggest obstacle in the entire implementation. Some projects have literally gone dead in the water when the magnitude of the interfacing job was discovered too late.

Here's a word of warning to the DP folks from someone who used to work there, and who's been down the MRP II implementation path many times: Don't underestimate the interfacing task. During the cost justification process, consider the existing applications and the most likely software packages. Try to get a rough-cut estimate of interfacing man-hours (or days, or weeks, or months). When in doubt, lean towards the high side.

Then, when it is time to select the software, choose the route of least *pain*. The ideal here is simple software, easy to interface. Another colleague, John DeVito from the great state of Texas, points out that the price of a software package is only one element of software costs. John's formula is that the total initial cost of software—equals:

Purchase Price
+
Modification Costs
+
Interface Costs
+
Delay Costs

DP's challenge is to minimize the total costs.

5. *Save the Pockets of Excellence.* Many companies do some things very well. An example of this would be a company with an excellent shop floor control system, but very little else. The computer part of this system may have been programmed in-house, and may contain some helpful features for the users. (Some companies do many of these things very well, and these are candidates for writing the rest of their own software.)

Let's assume further the MRP II software package selected by this company contains a workable set of programs for shop floor control, but not as good as the company's current system. This company should not blindly proceed to replace its superior shop floor control system with the new, inferior one. That kind of move could severely damage operational performance and user morale.

Save the good stuff. Don't throw the baby out with the bath water.

6. *Beware of Plain Vanilla.* Some companies attempt to implement MRP II with the software "as is"—with no modifications. Their plan is to go back and make the changes after the system is up and running.

Why bother? If the system's working, there's no real need to modify it. Almost invariably, however, the software needs to be modified *before* implementation, just to make it work properly in the first place. What are the chances a given set of software, encompassing all of the functions of MRP II, can be implemented properly in a given company without modification? Two chances: slim and none.

Remember, MRP II implementation is not some kind of low-grade computer project. It's a matter of *changing the way the business is run* to allow major improvements in *how well* the business is run.

Managing Requests for Changes

If modifications are going to be necessary, where does a company draw the line? How do they keep from being inundated with requests for changes?

Good question. This can be a real problem. Three elements come into play: education, standard software, and management.

Requests for changes will be minimized if the company does a good job of MRP II *education*. This will help the users think of solving their problems within the overall framework of MRP II. Add to this a set of *standard software*, relatively complete in terms of functionality. Then, what the users learn about MRP II will be reflected in the software. However, even with excellent education and good software, requests for software modification will still be forthcoming. This is where *effective management* enters the picture.

Key people, particularly members of the steering committee and project team, need to recognize two principles:

1. *Resist changes.* The mind set of these folks should be one of resisting any changes to the software which are not essential for either running the business and/or implementing MRP II. They need to understand that too many changes can delay the project. Thus they may be very expensive, based on the cost of a one-month delay. Further, they may reduce the odds for real success with MRP II, because long, stretched-out implementations are less likely to succeed.

2. *Distinguish between systems which are "computer-essential" and those which are "automated manual."* Systems such as MRP, CRP and shop floor control are computer-essential; they simply cannot be done manually, because of the enormous volume of calculations involved. Ollie had a good way of putting it: "To do material requirements planning manually in most companies would require a staff about the size of the Chinese army plus a year's output from the Eagle pencil factory."

Automated manual systems are ones like payroll, general ledger, billing, automating the printing of purchase orders, etc. They can be done manually. Although computerizing these activities may be beneficial, the key is that they can be done effectively without the computer.

Automated manual systems have had great impact in fields such as banking and insurance where the "direct labor force," so to speak, is clerical office workers. In manufacturing companies, the big paybacks have come from computer-essential systems, such as the ones which are the subject of this book.

Those are the principles. Here's a good approach to the process:

1. The data processing department is geared up to provide a certain amount of modifications, changes, enhancements, etc. The necessary funds have been budgeted in the cost justification.

2. Requests for modifications are submitted to data processing for an evaluation of the *amount* of work involved. A dividing line of X man-hours of systems/programming time is established to distinguish between major and minor modifications. (Obviously, X will vary from company to company.) Data processing's evaluation places the requested modification into either the major or minor category.

Note: Data processing personnel do not decide on the appropriateness or the need for the change. They're free to comment, but do not make that decision.

3. The request then goes to the project team. If the request is for a minor change, the project team decides whether to grant the request (do it soon), refuse it (it's not necessary), or to defer the change to Phase III. (Back in Chapter 3, I identified Phase III as being made up of finance and simulation, plus other elements judged as desirable but not essential for MRP II.)

4. If the request is for a major change, the project team reviews it and makes a recommendation. The key issue here: Is this change *necessary* in order to continue to run the business and/or for MRP II to work properly? Does the function in question require the computer, or can it be done manually? If yes, it must be done now, or at least soon. If it's *desirable but not essential,* defer it to Phase III. (Sometimes the outside MRP II counsel can be helpful in putting these issues into focus.) The project team then forwards the request to the executive steering committee along with its recommendation.

5. At times, there can be a disagreement between the person requesting the change and the project team. In this case, the requester should be able to address the steering committee, presenting the request and the reasons for it. Hence he has his "day in court" and it's up to him to sell the steering committee on the merits of his request.

When handled in this manner, the "modification mountain" begins to shrink into a manageable molehill.

One last word about changes to the software. The conventional wisdom says: "Make changes on the front end or the back end, but don't make changes to the main internal logic of the programs themselves." I agree, provided it's possible. Sometimes, however, it's the internal logic that's flawed and requires the change. Examples of such problems include: computer control over the master schedule, not using the rescheduling assumption in material requirements planning, improper back scheduling logic in shop floor control, etc. The easiest solution to these problems is to choose software with valid logic. When that choice is not possible, it may be necessary to get into the internal "guts" of the programs and make the necessary changes.

An additional discussion of software maintenance issues can be found in Chapter 11, Operating MRP II.

Chapter 9 will address the issue of "turning on" the first phase of MRP II. It's taken a lot of work to get this far—education and training, data integrity and policy statements, software acquisition. But remember—the clock has been ticking only *less* than a year.

IMPLEMENTERS' CHECKLIST

Function: SOFTWARE & SYSTEMS

Task	Complete	
	Yes	No
1. Decision made to "make" (write) or "buy" software for MRP II.	____	____
2. If buying, the software package selected has been shown to be operating at a Class A or high Class B level.	____	____
3. The magnitude of the internal systems and programming workload (new programs, interfacing, etc.) has been estimated and provided for in the cost justification.	____	____
4. Procedures to manage requests for changes to the software established and in place.	____	____

Going on the Air—Phase I

"Going on the air" with a system means turning it on, starting to run it. It's the culmination of a great deal of work done to date.

Back in Chapter 3, I discussed the proper implementation sequence: basic MRP, closed loop MRP, MRP II. This approach is clearly shown on the *Proven Path* chart, and it may be helpful to refer to it occasionally throughout this chapter.

Basic MRP

Basic MRP consists of production planning, master production scheduling, rough-cut capacity planning, material requirements planning, anticipated delay feedback from the shop floor and purchasing, and distribution resource planning where applicable. The supporting elements of sales forecasting, customer order entry, bill of material processing, and inventory transaction processing are also involved here. Let's start with the first one.

PRODUCTION PLANNING

As I've said repeatedly throughout this book, the people responsible for implementing a given function must be the ones who will operate it after it is implemented. This is as true with production planning as with every other function within MRP II, and it's no less true here. Therefore, since top management is accountable for *operating* production planning, they must be the ones to implement it. See Figure 9-1.

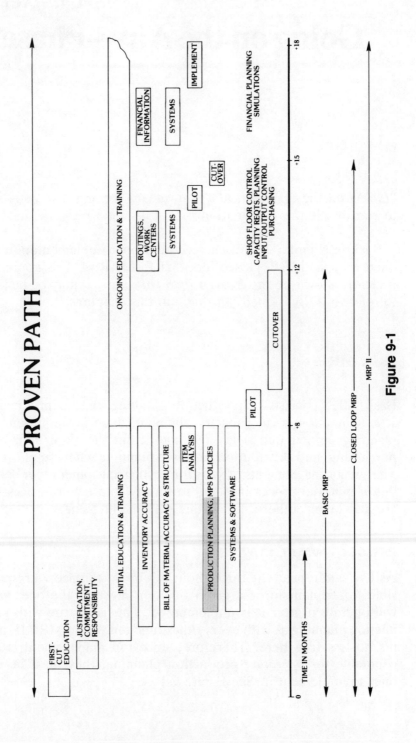

Figure 9-1

This identifies another "reason for being" for the executive steering committee. In addition to their responsibilities for leadership, resource allocation, breaking bottlenecks, etc., this group will be responsible for implementing production planning. They'll probably need some help from people at the operating level in getting the necessary numbers on sales, production, inventories, and backlog. They may also need some input regarding product families, etc. But the responsibility is ultimately theirs. (A fine tool to help in this process is "The Production Planning Starter Kit," available from R.D. Garwood, Inc., P.O. Box 28755, Atlanta, GA 30328.)

Production planning should be implemented just as soon as practical—certainly some months before MPS/MRP. There are three reasons for this timing: learning curve, benefits, and example.

As with most things, there's a definite *learning curve* involved with production planning. The first time probably won't go very well. The second time will be better than the first, the third better than the second, and so on. The catch is there's only one opportunity per month to do production planning, so it's important to start as soon as possible. Once everyone on the executive steering committee has been through outside education, have some inside education sessions on production planning. Start to do production planning at that time. In that way, there'll be education, training and implementation going on simultaneously. And that's fine.

One of my associates, Andre Martin, was formerly the director of manufacturing and materials management at Abbott Laboratories Canada. He was also torchbearer during their superb implementation of MRP II. Andre says: "It took Abbott Canada nine months to become truly effective in the production planning process."

Many companies have experienced some positive *benefits* from operating production planning alone, before MPS/MRP. For perhaps the first time, the top executives in the company are sitting down once a month, focusing on the performance of sales, production, inventories and backlogs, and making decisions for the future. In many companies, this process alone will start to make things better.

Last but not least is the importance of setting an *example*. Leadership and example are closely intertwined. People throughout the company will be happy to see that not only is top management getting educated, but that they are already in implementation and operation mode. They'll feel reassured about that. As a result, morale should rise and enthusiasm build.

SUPPORTING ELEMENTS

All of the supporting elements must be in place prior to going on the air with MPS/MRP. Material requirements planning can't be run without accurate inventory records, accurate and properly structured bills of material, shop floor and purchasing feedback, and a valid master production schedule. The master schedule can't be valid without sales forecasts, customer order data, product load profiles (for rough-cut capacity planning), etc.

The company needs all of this data, as well as the information described in the preceding chapter. New software may be necessary to get and maintain the data. And *written* operating policies as discussed in Chapter 7 are also required.

MASTER PRODUCTION SCHEDULING/MATERIAL REQUIREMENTS PLANNING

Here is the second "moment of truth" during implementation. (The first was the point of commitment to the project.) Virtually all the company's activities to date have been leading directly to activating MPS/MRP. Turning these on can be very tricky, and we need to discuss at length how to do it.

Three Ways to Implement Systems

THE PARALLEL APPROACH

There are, broadly, three different approaches to implementing systems. One is the *parallel* approach. It means continuing to run the old system after the new system is running. The output from the new system is compared to the old. When the new system proves it is consistently giving the correct answers, the old system is dropped.

There are two problems in using the parallel method for MRP. First of all, it's difficult. It's very cumbersome to maintain and operate two systems side by side. There may not be enough staff to do all of that and still have time left over to do the comparison of the new system output to the old.

The second problem with the parallel approach is perhaps even more compelling than the first: it's *impossible*. The essence of the parallel approach is the comparison of the output from the new system against the old system. The new system in this case is basic MRP. But against *what* should its output be compared? The Kardex cards? The order point system? The stock status report? The HARP[1] system? What's the point of implementing MRP II if it's just going to deliver the same kind of lousy information that's been available all along from the current system?

That's the problem with the parallel approach for MRP. For implementing accounting systems, as an example, it's great. It's the way to do it because *current accounting systems work.*

Pre-MRP systems in the field of manufacturing logistics did not really work, so they can't be used as a standard for comparison.

COLD TURKEY

This dilemma leads some people to jump all the way to the other end of the spectrum and use a method called *cold turkey* cutover. I call it "you bet your company," and I recommend against it vigorously and without reservation.

Here's an example of a cold turkey implementation, as explained by an unenlightened project leader:

[1] HARP is an acronym for Half-Assed Requirements Planning. Many people who think they have MRP actually have HARP: monthly time buckets, requirements generated every month or so, etc. It's a primitive order launcher, which does happen to recognize the principle of independent/dependent demand.

"We've got MPS and MRP all programmed, tested, and de-
bugged. We're going to run it live over the weekend. On
Friday afternoon, we're going to back a pick-up truck into
the production control office, throw all fifty thousand Kardex
cards in the truck and take 'em down to the incinerator."

This might be called "burning one's Kardex," a variation of
burning one's bridges behind one. A cold turkey implementation
places the company in an absolutely unacceptable degree of risk.
Some companies that do a cold turkey may actually lose their
ability to order material and parts. The old system can't help
them, because they stopped running it. MRP can't help them if
it's not working properly. Perhaps the output isn't valid, or maybe
it's so voluminous that the people are simply overwhelmed. By
the time they realize the seriousness of the problem, they often
can't go back to the old system, because the inventory balances
and other data are no longer current. (Even those cases when
they can go back to the old system are very unfortunate. Why?
Because they tried to implement MRP, and it didn't work. Probably they got overwhelmed. Now they're back to running the old
system, not MRP, and they'll have to decide what to do now,
where to go from here. A most unfortunate situation.)
  A company that can't order material and parts will sooner or
later lose its ability to ship product. A company that can't ship
product will, sooner or later, no longer be in business.
  Some organizations get lucky and muddle through without great
difficulty. In other cases, it's far more serious. While I'm not
aware of any company which has actually gone out of business
for this reason, there are some who've come close. None of the
people I've talked to who've lived through a cold turkey cutover
say they would want to do it again. Don't do it.

THE PILOT APPROACH

The right way to do it is with a *pilot*. This involves selecting a
group of products, or one product, or a part of one product—
involving no more than several hundred part numbers in all—
and doing a cold turkey on those. The purpose is to *prove* that

MRP works before cutting over all five thousand or fifty thousand or five hundred thousand items onto the system. The phrase "MRP works" refers to two things: the technical side (does the software work properly?) and the users' side (do the people understand and believe what it's telling them, and do they know what to do?).

If MRP doesn't work properly during the pilot, it's not a major problem. All of the parts are still being ordered via the old system, except for the few hundred in the pilot. These can be handled by putting them back on the old system, or perhaps doing them manually. What's also necessary is to focus on *why* MRP isn't working properly and fix it. The people have the time to do that if they're not being inundated with output on five thousand or fifty thousand or five hundred thousand parts.

What do I mean when I say "Is it working?" Simply, is it predicting the shortages? Is it generating correct recommendations to release orders, and to reschedule orders in and out? Does the master schedule for the pilot product(s) reflect what's actually being made? Can customer orders be promised with confidence? Answering "yes" to those kinds of questions means it's working.

Three Kinds of Pilots

"Doing it right" means using three different types of pilots. They're the computer pilot, the conference room pilot and the live pilot.

1. The *computer pilot* simply means checking out the software very thoroughly. If a company has written its own, this means testing and debugging. If they've bought software, it means running the programs on the computer, and debugging them. (Remember, there *will* be bugs in the software, no matter whether it's home-grown or purchased.) This process should begin as soon as the programs are available.

Often, the computer pilot will deal initially with "dummy" items and "dummy" data. In purchased software, this should come as part of the package. The dummy products are things like bicycles, pen and pencil sets, etc., and the dummy data are transactions made up to test the programs. Then, if practical, run the new programs using "real" data from the company, using as much data as can readily be put into the system. The objective of the computer pilot is to ensure the software works on the computer and to learn more about it. The key players are the systems and data processing staff, usually with some help from one or more project team members. See Figure 9-2 for the "location" of the computer pilot.

2. *The conference room pilot* follows the computer pilot. The main objectives of the conference room pilot are education and training: for the users to learn more about the software, to learn how to use it and to manage their part of the business with it, and to make sure it fits the business. This process can also help to establish procedures and to identify areas that may require policy directions. As indicated in Figure 9-3, the emphasis has shifted from the computer to the people.

The key people involved are the users, primarily the master scheduler(s) and the material planners. The items involved are "real world" items, normally the ones which will be involved in the live pilot. The data, however, will be *dummy* data, for two reasons:

a. Live data shouldn't be used because the company's still not yet ready to run this thing for real. Everyone's still in "learning and testing" mode.

b. It's important to "exercise" the total system (people as well as software) just as much as possible. Some of the dummy data for the conference room pilot should be "manufactured" so it will present as many challenges as possible to the people and the software.

One "exercise technique" that works very nicely is for a key person, perhaps the project leader, to play "Murphy" (as in Murphy's Law). As the conference room pilot is being operated, "Murphy" periodically appears and scraps out an entire lot of production, or becomes a vendor who'll be three weeks late shipping, or causes a machine to go down, or generates a mandatory and immediate engineering change.

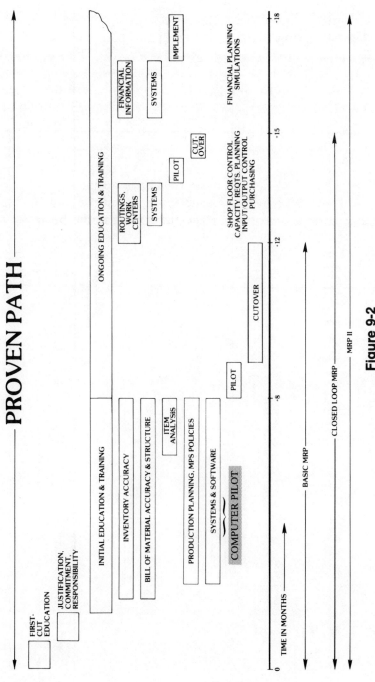

Figure 9-2

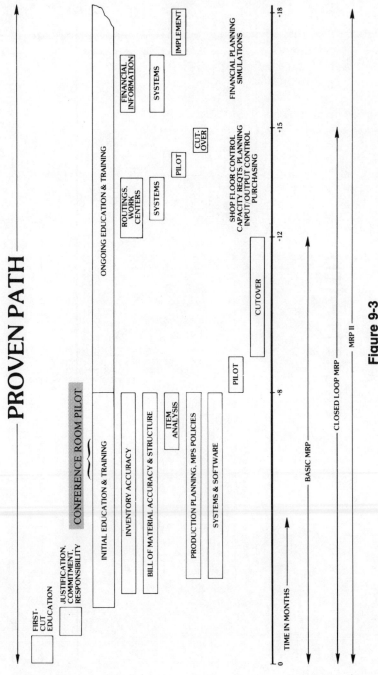

Figure 9-3

Presenting the people and the software with these kinds of challenges will pay dividends in the live pilot and cutover stages. One company that Walt Goddard worked with used a slogan during the conference room pilot: "MAKE IT FAIL." Super! This is another version of "bulletproofing." During the conference room phase, they worked hard at exposing the weak spots, finding the problems, making it fail. The reason: so that in the live pilot phase, *it would work.*

The conference room pilot should be run until the users really know the system. Here are two good tests for readiness:

a. Ask the users, before they enter a transaction into the system, what the results of that transaction will be. When they can routinely predict what will result, they know the system well.

b. Select several MPS and MRP output reports (or screens) at random. Ask the users to explain what every number on the page means, why it's there, how it got there, etc. When they can do that routinely, they've got a good grasp of what's going on.

If the prior steps have been done correctly and the supporting elements are in place, the conference room pilot shouldn't take more than a month or so.

3. The *live pilot* is that moment of truth I mentioned earlier. It's when master scheduling and material requirements planning go into operation for the first time in the real world. See Figure 9-4.

The objective of the live pilot is to *prove* MPS and MRP will work within the company. Until then, that can't be said. All that one could say up to that point are things like "it should work," "we think it'll work," "it really ought to work," etc. Only after the live pilot has been run successfully can the people say "it works."

Before I get into the details of the live pilot, let me recap what I've covered so far by taking a look at Figure 9-5.

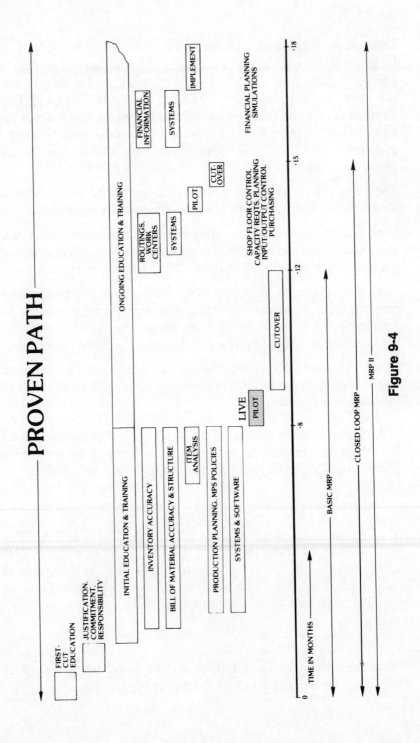

PROVEN PATH

Figure 9-4

Figure 9-5 The Three Types of Pilots

Type	Key People	Items/Data	Objective
Computer	Data Processing Selected Project Team Members	Dummy/Dummy	1. Run the software on the computer and debug it 2. Learn more about the software
Conference Room	Master Scheduler(s) Material Planners Selected Project Team Members Data Processing	Live/Dummy	1. Enable the room users to learn the software thoroughly 2. Verify that the software fits the business
Live	Master Scheduler(s) Material Planners	Live/Live	1. Prove the system works 2. Obtain a sign-off from the users

Selecting the Live Pilot

What are the criteria for a good live pilot? Some of the considerations are:

1. *Size.* It requires enough items to get a good test of how the overall man/machine system performs, but not so many times as to get overwhelmed. A good rule of thumb is to use somewhere between two hundred and six hundred items.

2. *Product Orientation.* The pilot should represent all of the items for an entire product family (in the case of a simple product, such as clothing or cosmetics), or a single product (moderately complex products, like bicycles or typewriters), or a part of a product (highly complex products, such as aircraft or machine tools). In the latter example, the pilot might be one "leg" in the bill of materials, or perhaps a modular planning bill for an option.

3. *Good Cross-section.* The pilot group should contain a good mix of finished products (or a portion thereof), subassemblies or intermediates, manufactured items, purchased items and raw materials.

4. *Relatively Self-contained.* The fewer "common parts" contained in the pilot, the better. Items used in both the pilot product and others will not give a good test of MRP. MRP will not be aware of all of the requirements for those items. The usual way of handling these is to post the MRP-generated requirements back to the old system. Some degree of commonality is almost always present (raw materials, in many cases) but try to pick a pilot where it's at a minimum.

5. *Best Planner.* If the company has material planners already and they're organized on a product basis, try to run the pilot on the product handled by the best planner. This is a people-intensive process, and it needs to have just as much going for it as possible.

LOOK BEFORE YOU LEAP

Let's consider what has to be in place prior to the live pilot. One element is a successful conference room pilot, where the users have proven they understand the system thoroughly. The other key elements are data integrity and education and training. Please refer to the Implementers' Checklist at the end of this chapter.

The project team should address the first six entries on the checklist. All must be answered "Yes." The project leader then reports the results to the executive steering committee and asks for formal permission to launch the live pilot. Only after that's received should they proceed.

OPERATING THE LIVE PILOT

When everything's in place and ready to go, start running the pilot items on MPS/MRP and stop running them on the old system. The objectives are to prove MPS/MRP is working, and to obtain user sign-off. Is it predicting the shortages, giving correct recommendations, and so forth? Are the users, the master scheduler(s) and the material planners, making the proper responses and taking the correct action? Are the users prepared to state formally that they can run their part of the business with these tools? If the users are unwilling and/or unable to sign-off on the system, then one of several factors is probably present:

- It's not working properly.
- They don't understand it.
- Both of the above.

In any of these cases, the very worst thing would be to proceed into the cutover phase—to put all of the remaining items onto the new system. First, aggressively go after the problem: either fix the system that's not working properly, or correct the deficiency in education and training that's causing the user not to understand it, or both.

Run the live pilot as long as it takes.

Don't go beyond the pilot stage until it's working and the users have signed off. This is one area where the aggressive implementation mentality must take a back seat. Everyone—executive steering committee, project team, users—should understand the company won't go beyond the live pilot until it's been proven to work and until the users are comfortable with it.

Plan to run the live pilot for about a month, or longer if manufacturing cycles are long and speeds are slow. It's essential to observe how the man/machine system performs over a number of weeks to prove it really works. A week is not enough time. A quarter is probably too long, for planning purposes, for most companies.

During the live pilot, don't neglect training. Get the other planning people as close to the pilot operation as possible, without getting in the way of the folks who are operating it. People not involved in the pilot need all the input they can get, because they'll be on the firing line soon, when the rest of the parts are cut over to MRP II.

Cutover

Once the live pilot is working well, and the users are comfortable with it, it's time to cutover the rest of the items onto the MPS/ MRP system. See Figure 9-6.

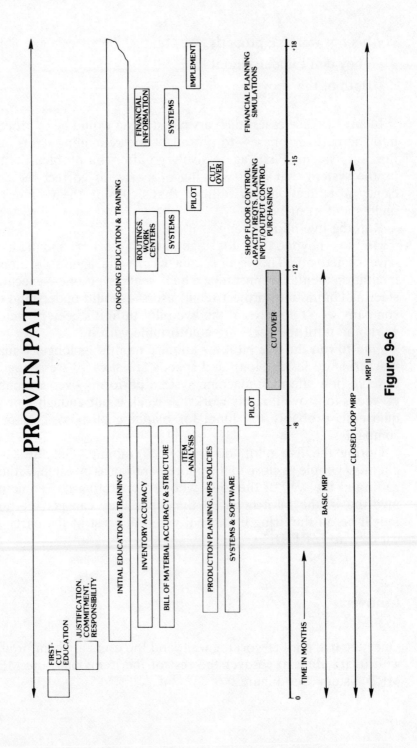

PROVEN PATH

FIRST-CUT EDUCATION

JUSTIFICATION, COMMITMENT, RESPONSIBILITY

ONGOING EDUCATION & TRAINING

INITIAL EDUCATION & TRAINING

INVENTORY ACCURACY

BILL OF MATERIAL ACCURACY & STRUCTURE

ITEM ANALYSIS

PRODUCTION PLANNING, MPS POLICIES

SYSTEMS & SOFTWARE

PILOT

CUTOVER

ROUTINGS, WORK CENTERS

SYSTEMS

PILOT

CUT-OVER

SHOP FLOOR CONTROL
CAPACITY REQTS. PLANNING
INPUT/OUTPUT CONTROL
PURCHASING

FINANCIAL INFORMATION

SYSTEMS

IMPLEMENT

FINANCIAL PLANNING
SIMULATIONS

TIME IN MONTHS

0   -8   +12   +15   +18

BASIC MRP

CLOSED LOOP MRP

MRP II

Figure 9-6

There are two different ways to cutover the remaining items. It can either be done in one large group or the remaining items can be divided into several groups and cutover one at a time.

The "divide and conquer" route is preferable because it has the following advantages:

1. It's less risky. It represents a more controlled process.

2. It's easier on the people. If the first group to cutover belongs to Planner A, then Planners B and C should be deeply involved in helping Planner A. It reduces Planner A's workload, and also provides additional training for B and C. When Planner B cuts over, Planners A and C can help *him*.

The multiple-group approach, on the other hand, may not always be practical and/or necessary. In some companies, the "common parts" situation is so widespread that it's very difficult to isolate groups. This means that, during the cutover process, many items will be partially but not totally on the new system. The difficulties in passing requirements from the new system to the old (or vice versa) can easily outweigh the benefits gained from using multiple groups. In this case, the one-group approach would probably be best. It's usually far better at this point to move ahead quickly than to spend lots of time and effort transferring requirements for common parts.

Sometimes the multiple-group approach may not even be necessary. A company with only a few thousand part numbers may validly conclude their entire population of items is small enough, and there's no real need to break it down any finer.

The Need for Feedback During Cutover

There's a potential dilemma here:

• This cutover is a Phase I activity. The MPS and MRP planning tools are being made operational.

- MPS and MRP can't function effectively by themselves. They're merely components of an overall closed loop system.
- However, closing the loop is a Phase III activity, to come later. How can MPS and MRP be "made operational" (i.e., work properly) prior to that?

The answer is that there must be a form of "loop closing" even during Phase I. It's essential. Without feedback from the plant and purchasing, the planning people won't be notified when jobs won't be completed on schedule. They must have that feedback or *they will not be able to keep the order dates valid.*

Therefore, anticipated delay reporting from both the plant and purchasing must be implemented as a part of Phase I. However, there's even a bit more to it than that.

At this point, the company's beginning to operate with the formal priority planning system (MPS/MRP), but doesn't yet have the priority execution system (the dispatching portion of shop floor control) in place. Given good feedback, order due dates can be kept valid and up-to-date, but the tools to communicate those changing priorities to the shop floor still aren't available. Further, without CRP, there's no specific, detailed visibility into future overloads and underloads at all of the work centers on the shop floor.

A good approach here is to develop an interim, possibly crude, shop scheduling system. It's used to get the job done until the full-blown shop floor control system is on the air. This interim system is usually manual, not computerized, and operates with order due dates and possibly a simplified back scheduling approach. (Example 1: Job #A has a four-week lead time. It's due two weeks from now. It should be 50% finished. Is it 50% finished? If not, it should be given priority. Example 2: Backschedule from the order due date assuming all operations take the same amount of time. Set operation due dates accordingly.)

In addition, it's highly desirable to assign one or more shop people full-time to the project during this transition phase. This person's responsibility is to help the folks on the plant floor work on the right jobs. This person maintains close contact with the interim shop scheduling system, with the material planners, and with the foremen. He finds out about the reschedules coming from the planners, makes sure the foremen are up to date, generates the anticipated delay report for the planners, helps break bottlenecks, etc.

The last point, breaking bottlenecks, brings up another post-cutover issue: overloads and underloads. This can be a problem because capacity requirements planning isn't operational yet. Overloads are bad, because the work won't get through on time. Underloads are almost as bad because people will run out of work, and get a very negative feeling about MRP II.

Once again, that key shop person mentioned earlier can be a big help—by "eyeballing" the queues, talking to the foremen about their problems, talking to the material planners about what MRP II shows is coming soon, breaking the bottlenecks, making certain the shop doesn't run out of work, etc. During this tricky transition period, do whatever possible to anticipate problems. Identifying them ahead of time can minimize their impact.

The buyers have a similar role to play with their vendors. They need to follow up closely with their vendors, learn which orders the vendors will not be able to ship on time, and communicate these to the planners via the anticipated delay report.

There's also a potential capacity problem with vendors. Since MRP is now involved in planning orders, the orders might not be coming out in the same pattern as before. The company could inadvertently be creating severe overloads or, just as bad perhaps, severe underloads at key vendors. The buyers need to stay in close contact with vendors, to solve these kinds of problems should they arise.

The three most important things the people can do during this period are:

1. Communicate
2. Communicate
3. Communicate

Talk to each other. Don't relax. Keep the groups—steering committee and project team—meeting at least as frequently as before, perhaps more frequently. Consider creating a spin-off task force to focus solely on these transitional problems, meeting perhaps every day.

Cutover is a very intense period. Plan to work long, long hours, and to make additional resources available. The project leader should be present constantly, "carrying the water bucket" and helping the users in any way he can. That also applies to the assistant project leader, if there is one, the department head (P & IC manager or whatever), and the key system people. Don't overwhelm the planners. Rather, overwhelm the *problems*. Get through all of the output. Take all the necessary actions. Make it work. Begin to measure performance. (See Chapter 11, Operational Measurements.)

THE POTENTIAL INVENTORY BLIP

What's the number one priority when implementing MRP II? Is it to reduce the inventories? Nope, that's not even number two. Number one priority, of course, is to run the business. Number two is to implement Manufacturing Resource Planning. Reducing inventories, *during the implementation process,* probably isn't even in the Top Five or Ten.

Should inventories start to drop during implementation? Towards the end, they should. But beware, *they may go up before they go down.* In a given company there's probably a fifty-fifty chance that this will happen.

Here's why.

When the company starts to run material requirements planning, its logic will identify a certain number of reschedule-ins and reschedule-outs. These would be for the scheduled receipts, both open shop orders and open purchase orders. Some will be needed sooner, some later. The logic of MRP will also recognize items that are needed, but for which there is no scheduled receipt. It will recommend releasing a new order.

What the logic of MRP will not do is make recommendations about *inventory already in the stockroom.* It's in the on-hand balance; it can't be rescheduled out, because it's already in stock. It'll probably be needed, but not until later. This phenomenon will cause some companies, in the short run, to expedite more than they're able to de-expedite. That introduces the possibility of a temporary inventory rise. See Figure 9-7.

Be aware this may happen. It's not illegal, immoral, or fattening. It should be anticipated. Then if it doesn't happen, so much the better.

DON'T STARVE THE SOURCES

Inventories that drop too *quickly* can also be a problem. A sharp drop in the inventory level may be an indication the implementation job is not being done properly.

The problem is the potential for "starving out" the shop and/or some key vendors because less work is being released to them. This can be especially likely to happen in companies that had far too much inventory before implementation. After basic MRP is on the air, material requirements planning will indicate there is far less need for parts or raw material. Therefore, relatively few new orders are released to the shop and vendors. These people, who have become accustomed to a regular flow of work over the years, now see very few orders.

Consider how a shop foreman or key vendor would feel in this situation. After hearing all the talk about how great MRP II is going to be, the first thing that happens is that orders dry up, and there's no work. MRP II will have a lot of negative impressions to live down in this case, and these first impressions may be lasting ones.

My message is: don't lose sight of this issue during cutover and risk starving the shop and/or the key vendors. If necessary, be prepared to release work early to keep the flow of work coming to them. The necessary adjustments to workloads, and therefore,

Figure 9-7 What Might Happen To Your Inventories

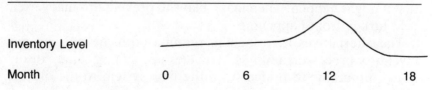

Inventory Level

| Month | 0 | 6 | 12 | 18 |

inventories, can then be made gradually over a longer period, without turning these vital sources of supply against MRP II.

THE INADVERTENT COLD TURKEY CUTOVER

Here's a potential booby trap. Some companies have accidentally "backed into" a cold turkey cutover, as follows:

1. They need to implement a new inventory transaction processing system, in order to reach 95% inventory accuracy.

2. They need to do this prior to going on the air with MRP. This is proper, since all of the records must be made accurate first.

3. The current inventory system contains *ordering logic;* it gives them signals of when to reorder. However, the new inventory transaction processing software is a module of an overall software package for MRP II. As such, there is no ordering logic in the inventory processor, whose function is to maintain inventory balances. The ordering logic is contained within a module called MRP.

4. The company implements the new inventory processor, and simultaneously discontinues using the old one.

5. The result is the company has lost its ability to order material and parts.

The wrong solution: discover this too late, scramble, and plug in the new software module which contains the ordering logic (MRP). The result is to implement MRP across the board, untested, with the likelihood of inaccurate inventory records, bad bills, a suspect master schedule and inadequate user education, training, and buy-in. The ultimate cold turkey cutover.

The right solution to this problem is to recognize ahead of time that it might happen. Then make plans to prevent this inadvertent cold turkey from happening.

The alternatives here include running both the old and new inventory processors until MRP comes up, writing some "throwaway" programs to bridge from the new system to the old, or, worst case, developing an interim set of ordering logic to be used during this period.

This concludes our discussion of implementing basic MRP. Remember, at this point, the company really doesn't have a complete operating system. There's urgency to close the loop completely, and that'll be covered in the next chapter.

IMPLEMENTERS' CHECKLIST

Function: GOING ON THE AIR—PHASE I

Task	Complete	
	Yes	No
1. Production planning implemented early on.	____	____
2. MPS/MRP pilot selected.	____	____
3. Computer pilot completed.	____	____
4. Conference room pilot completed.	____	____
5. Necessary levels of data accuracy—95% minimum on inventory records, 98% minimum on bills—still in place on *all* items, not merely the pilot items.	____	____
6. Initial education and training at least 80% complete throughout the company.	____	____
7. Executive steering committee authorization to start the live pilot.	____	____
8. Live pilot successfully operated, and user sign-off obtained.	____	____
9. Feedback links (anticipated delay reports) in place for both plant and purchasing.	____	____
10. Interim shop floor control system in place.	____	____
11. One or more shop people assigned full time to project during cutover.	____	____
12. Executive steering committee authorization to cutover.	____	____
13. Cutover onto MPS/MRP complete.	____	____

Chapter 10

Going on the Air— Phases II & III

Phase II involves acquiring closed loop MRP, both in manufacturing and purchasing. Phase III covers the financial interface and the simulation capability.

Closing the Loop in Manufacturing

Let's talk first about two issues that deal with the overall approach: sequence and timing. See Figure 10-1. I recommend you implement in the following sequence:

1. Shop Floor Control (Dispatching).
2. Capacity Requirements Planning.
3. Input/Output Control.

Shop floor control comes first because, as mentioned earlier, it's urgent to communicate those changing priorities out to the shop floor. Until it's possible to do that via the dispatching system, the company will have to live with the interim system. In all likelihood, that will be somewhat cumbersome, time consuming and less than completely efficient.

Capacity requirements planning comes next. It's less urgent. Also, when rough-cut capacity planning was implemented as a part of basic MRP, the company probably began to learn more about future capacity requirements than ever before.

Input/output control has to follow CRP. Input/output tracks actual performance to the capacity plan. The capacity plan (from CRP) must be in place before input/output control can operate.

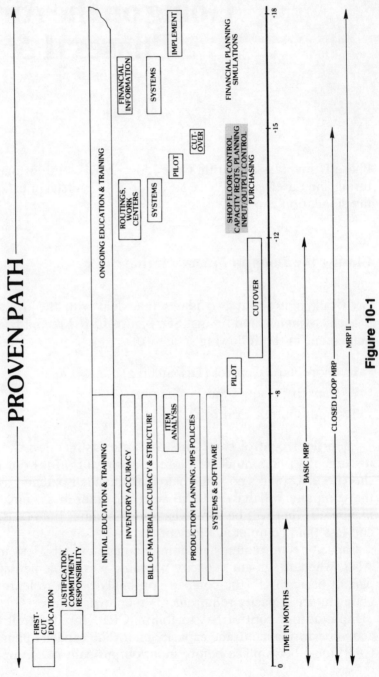

Figure 10-1

SPECIAL SITUATIONS

Here are two cases where closing the loop in manufacturing becomes real easy.

Case 1: The company has it all, or most of it, already. Some companies implemented shop floor control years before they ever heard of MRP II. This was frequently done in the mistaken belief that the causes of the problems—missed shipments, inefficiencies, excessive work-in-process inventories, etc.—were on the shop floor. Almost invariably, the *symptoms* are visible on the shop floor, but the *causes* get back to the lack of a formal priority planning system that works.

If most or all of the shop floor control/CRP tools are already working; that's super! In this case, closing the loop in manufacturing can occur just about simultaneously with cutover onto basic MRP. Several companies I've worked with had this happy situation, and it sure made life a lot easier.

A few words of caution. If you already have a shop floor control system and plan to keep it, don't assume that the data's accurate. Verify the accuracy of the routings, and the validity of the standards and work center data. Also, make certain that the system contains the standard shop floor control tools that have been proven to work, i.e., valid back scheduling logic, good order closeout tools, etc. The Standard System Description from Oliver Wight Software Research, Inc. can often help greatly in this evaluation.

Case 2: The company doesn't need all of it. If the manufacturing processes are purely in-line (flow shop) as opposed to functional (job shop), some of the shop floor control and CRP functions might not be necessary.

In a purely in-line process plant, there is often no need for shop dispatching because the line schedules are derived directly from the master production schedule. CRP may not be necessary, because rough-cut capacity planning can supply all the information needed about future requirements for capacity. Input/output control may give way to a simplified version of output tracking, where actual performance is compared to the planned requirements from rough-cut.

Pure flow shops, often called process or repetitive, are quite rare. Most plants are a combination of both job shop and flow shop. For plants which are strictly one or the other, the implementation job will be easier for the people in the flow shop than for their counterparts in the job shop. The software may need a bit of modification to deal with the absence of formal shop orders, to allow certain inventory accounts to be "backflushed," etc. Overall, however, the total MRP II system will be simpler, easier to implement, and easier to operate.

SHOP DATA COLLECTION

Shop data collection means collecting data from the shop. (How's that for real revelation?) It does not necessarily mean *automated* data collection, i.e., terminals on the shop floor with bells and whistles and flashing lights. This runs counter to what some of the computer hardware salesmen of this world would like their customers to believe. The shop data collection process doesn't have to be automated to operate closed loop MRP successfully. Some of the best shop floor control systems use paper and pencil as their data collection device, or perhaps a pencil and a pre-punched data processing card.

A company that already has automated data collection on the shop floor has a leg up. It should make the job easier. A company that doesn't have it now, but wants to do it as part of the MRP II project, can go ahead with implementing it, provided:

1. They can cost justify it, and
2. They can be sure that it won't delay the project.

If it'll slow down the project, do it later—after MRP II is on the air.

PILOT

I recommend a brief pilot of certain shop floor control activities. Quite a few procedures are going to be changing, and a lot of people are going to be involved. A 2–3 week pilot will help validate the procedures, the transactions, the software, and most importantly, the people's education and training.

It's usually preferable to pilot shop floor control with selected jobs, rather than selected work centers. With these few selected jobs moving through a variety of work centers, one can usually get a good handle on how well the basics are operating.

Note the use of the word "basics." The pilot will *not* be able to test the dispatch lists. Obviously, that won't be possible until after cutover, when all of the jobs are on the system.

CUTOVER

Once the pilot has proven the procedures, transactions, software, education and training, it's time for cutover. Here are the steps:

1. Load the shop status data into the computer.

2. Start to operate shop floor control and to use the dispatch list. Correct whatever problems pop up, fine tune the procedures and software as required, and make it work.

3. Begin running capacity requirements planning. Be careful— don't go out and buy a million dollars worth of new equipment based on the output of the first CRP run. Review the output carefully and critically. Get friendly with it. Within a few weeks, people should start to gain confidence in it and be able to use it to help manage this part of the business.

4. Start generating input/output reports. Establish the tolerances and define the ground rules for taking corrective action.

5. Start to measure shop performance, in terms of both priority and capacity. (See Chapter 11, Operational Measurements.)

Last, and perhaps most important of all, *don't neglect the feedback links.* Feedback is not a software module; it won't come as part of your software package. This is a verbal and handwritten person-to-person communication process. It will not involve the computer, except perhaps in very large companies, where a computer may possibly be used for message handling.

Feedback means things like foreman-to-foreman communication, daily foremen's meetings, the generation of anticipated delay reports, etc. The feedback links established in Phase I should be reviewed, tested, strengthened, made to work even better. The better the feedback, the better the closed loop system will operate. Without feedback, there is no closed loop.

Closing the Loop in Purchasing

Closing the loop in purchasing means implementing vendor scheduling. See Figure 10-2. Here's a simplified look at vendor scheduling:

1. Establish long-term contractual relationships with vendors.

2. Create a group of people (vendor schedulers) who are in direct contact with both vendors and MRP, eliminating purchase requisitions for production items.

3. Give vendors weekly schedules, eliminating hard copy purchase orders.

4. Get buyers out of "expedite and paperwork mode," freeing up their time to do the really important parts of their jobs: sourcing, negotiation, contracting, cost reduction, value analysis, etc.

Vendor scheduling should be implemented either simultaneously with shop floor control, CRP, and I/O or immediately after it. Most companies can do it simultaneously. Different people are involved: the foremen and some others for the shop systems, the buyers, vendor schedulers and vendors for the purchasing system.

If there is a resource conflict, it's often in data processing. Perhaps there's simply too much programming involved for both to be done simultaneously. In this situation, close the loop in manufacturing first, then do purchasing. Once again, it's urgent to bring up the shop floor control system, so changing priorities can be communicated effectively to the shop floor. Purchasing,

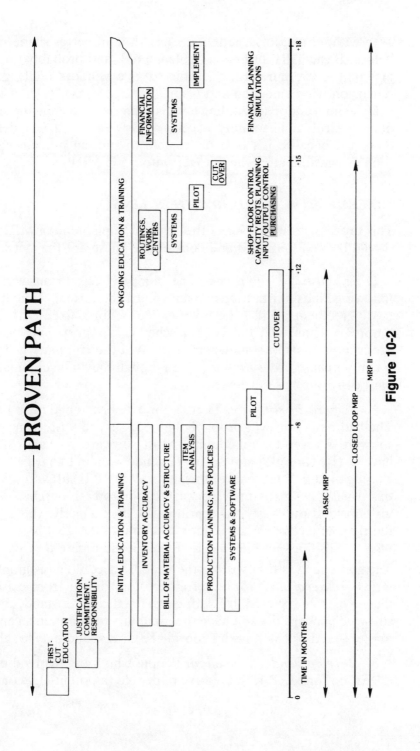

Figure 10-2

even without vendor scheduling, should be in better shape than before. Basic MRP has been implemented, and probably for the first time ever, purchasing is able to give vendors really good signals on what's needed and when.

Delaying vendor scheduling a bit is preferable to delaying shop floor control, if absolutely necessary. Try to avoid any delay, however, because it's best to be able to start in purchasing as soon as possible after the cutover onto basic MRP.

IMPLEMENTING VENDOR SCHEDULING

This process, as with every other part of implementing MRP II, should be well managed and controlled. These are the steps:

1. *Establish the approach.* The company has to answer the following kinds of questions: What will be the format of the business agreement? Will it be open-ended or for a fixed period of time? To whom will the vendor schedulers report: purchasing, production control, somewhere else? Will the company need to retain purchase order *numbers* even though they'll be eliminating hard copy purchase orders?

2. *Acquire the software.* There's good news and bad news here. The bad news is it will probably be necessary to write your own software for vendor scheduling. Most software packages don't have it. (Be careful: many software vendors claim to have a "purchasing module" as a part of their overall MRP II software. What this usually means is their package can automate purchase requisitions and purchase order printing. Unfortunately, this is not the right objective. With vendor scheduling, the goal is to *eliminate* requisitions and hard copy POs, not automate them.)

The good news is that writing the vendor scheduling programs is largely *retrieval and display* programming, drawn from existing files, which is typically less difficult. On the other hand, if the software package doesn't have the capability to maintain a vendor master file, the programming job will be correspondingly tougher.

3. *Develop vendor education.* People who'll be involved need education for MRP II. Vendors are people (a potentially controversial point in some companies that treat their vendors like dogs). Vendors will be involved. Therefore, vendors need education about MRP II.

Most companies who've had success with vendor scheduling have put together a one-day program for vendor education and training. The education part covers MRP II, how material requirements planning generates and maintains valid due dates, and why order due dates will be far better than ever before. The principle of "Silence is approval" must be explained thoroughly.

The training part gets at the vendor schedule, how to read it, when and how to respond, when to provide feedback, etc.

4. *Pilot with one vendor.* Select a vendor and get their concurrence in advance to participate in the vendor scheduling pilot. This vendor should supply substantial volume, should be cooperative, and, ideally, is located nearby. In the best of all possible worlds, this vendor would already be in "vendor scheduling mode" with one or more customers who have a Class A MRP II system.

Bring in their key people—plant manager, sales manager, key scheduling person, as well as their salesman. Educate them, train them and, in the same session, cut them over onto vendor scheduling.

5. *Fine tune the system.* Based on what's learned in this pilot, modify the approach if necessary, refine the education process, and tweak the software. Begin to measure performance.

6. *Educate and cutover the major vendors.* Go after the approximately 20% of the vendors who are supplying about 80% of the purchased volume. Get their tentative concurrence in advance. Bring them into the plan in groups of three to six vendors per day. Or, if necessary, go to their plant. As in the pilot, educate them, train them and cut them over on the same day.

If it isn't possible to get tentative concurrence in advance from a given vendor, attempt to convince them of vendor scheduling's benefits to them, as well as to the customer. Demonstrate how it's a "win-win" situation. Consider taking the one-day education session to their plant. If the vendor is still reluctant, involve the company president in direct contact with the vendor's president. (Carrying the water bucket is what presidents are for, right?) If all of these efforts fail, give them ninety days or so to shape up. Show them some positive results with other vendors already on vendor scheduling. If they're not getting cooperative by that time, start to look for a new vendor.

7. *Start to measure performance.* Start tracking vendor performance on delivery. Possibly for the first time ever, a company can *legitimately* hold vendors accountable for delivery performance—because probably for the first time ever, they can give vendors valid due dates.

Also, begin tracking buyer performance and vendor scheduler performance. (For more details, see Chapter 11, Operational Measurements.)

Communicate the measurements to everyone being measured. Raise the high bar—the level of expectation. When performance matches that, raise the bar again.

8. *Educate and cutover the remaining vendors.* As soon as the major vendors are on the air with vendor scheduling, go after the remainder. The target should be 100% of all suppliers of production items on vendor scheduling. It will probably take longer than the three months shown on the bar chart, but it's important to stick with it.

Implementing Finance and Simulation

If things have gone well up until now, these last two elements should not present a major problem. If things haven't gone well, fix what's wrong before trying to implement these tools. See Figure 10-3.

FINANCIAL PLANNING

Step one is to educate the people in finance and accounting early. Don't make the mistake of waiting until Month 12 or 14 to start

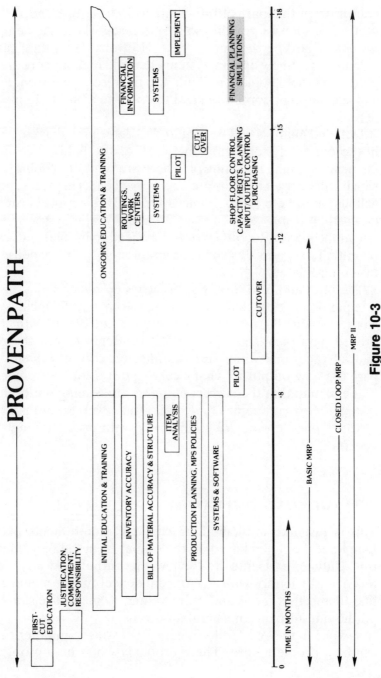

PROVEN PATH

FIRST-
CUT
EDUCATION

JUSTIFICATION,
COMMITMENT,
RESPONSIBILITY

INITIAL EDUCATION & TRAINING

ONGOING EDUCATION & TRAINING

INVENTORY ACCURACY

BILL OF MATERIAL ACCURACY & STRUCTURE

ITEM
ANALYSIS

PRODUCTION PLANNING, MPS POLICIES

SYSTEMS & SOFTWARE

PILOT

CUTOVER

ROUTINGS,
WORK
CENTERS

SYSTEMS

PILOT

CUT-
OVER

FINANCIAL
INFORMATION

SYSTEMS

IMPLEMENT

SHOP FLOOR CONTROL
CAPACITY REQTS. PLANNING
INPUT OUTPUT CONTROL
PURCHASING

FINANCIAL PLANNING
SIMULATIONS

TIME IN MONTHS

0   •8   •12   •15   •18

BASIC MRP

CLOSED LOOP MRP

MRP II

Figure 10-3

education in this part of the company. These folks need the education as soon as possible so they can see where the company's headed regarding the entire MRP II effort. Then they can participate effectively in the systems design, making sure the necessary financial "hooks" are built into the records early on. Finance and accounting people will need to do quite a bit of "homework" here.

Detailed analysis will be required to determine that each record in the overall system will contain all of the fields necessary for financial planning and control. These are typically "dollar" fields, which will be used to translate operational data (in pieces, pounds, gallons, liters, etc.) into financial terms. If this process isn't done early, then it may be necessary to make major systems changes late in the game. Record layouts may need to be changed, causing potentially a good deal of reprogramming, extra expense, confusion and delay.

The pilot and cold turkey approaches do *not* apply in this area. The parallel approach *does,* because the current financial systems work already. Naturally, they'll work a lot better with the improved data they'll get from MRP II. Begin to run the new financial programs while still running the current system. Compare the new output to what's coming out of the current system. Make certain that the correct numbers are coming out of the new system. Most companies find that, after several months of a satisfactory parallel, they're comfortable with discontinuing the old system.

IMPLEMENTING SIMULATION

This is just like implementing capacity requirements planning. Don't bet the ranch based on the output from the first simulation run. Rather, ease into it. Review the output critically—get familiar and friendly with it. As confidence builds, managers will find themselves more and more willing to make decisions based on the output from the simulation runs.

A word to the good folks in data processing: computer run time can be a problem here. There probably won't be a problem if:

- There are relatively few items and work centers, and/or
- The software contains net change MRP and CRP.

Many companies don't fit the above pattern. They have lots of items and lots of work centers. They have regenerative MRP, or CRP, or both.

Companies in this latter group need to scope out just how much of a potential problem the run time issue will be. If it's minor, then everything will probably be OK "as is." If major, they'll need to program their way around it. Generally this means making the regenerative CRP or MRP/CRP systems act like net change, probably via an approach called "requirements alteration."

The basic trade-off is computer run time versus programming effort. Step one is to determine if there's a run time problem. This may not be possible until after master scheduling, MRP and CRP have been implemented. Step two, if it proves out that run times will be a problem, is to get to work on programming around it.

There's no one detailed solution which will apply to all, or even most, companies. Variations in software, hardware, file sizes, and the magnitude of the run time problem preclude a clear-cut, widely applicable course of action. Therefore, an individualized solution will probably be required. In addition to a company's own systems and programming people, it may be necessary to get help from the software vendor's technical support people. Perhaps the MRP II consultant can be helpful, either directly or by making available other expertise.

Next up: what to do after the whole system is implemented. There are some very definite dos and don'ts regarding operating MRP II, which I'll get into in Chapter 11.

IMPLEMENTERS' CHECKLIST

Function: GOING ON THE AIR—PHASES II & III

Task	Complete Yes	No
1. Routing accuracy of 98% minimum for all items still in place.	——	——
2. Shop floor control pilot complete.	——	——
3. Shop floor control implemented across the board.	——	——
4. Dispatch list generating valid priorities.	——	——
5. Capacity requirements planning implemented.	——	——
6. Input/output control implemented.	——	——
7. Vendor education program developed.	——	——
8. Vendor scheduling pilot complete.	——	——
9. Major vendors cutover to vendor scheduling.	——	——
10. Measurement system implemented.	——	——
11. All vendors cutover to vendor scheduling.	——	——
12. Financial planning interfaces complete and implemented.	——	——
13. Simulation implemented.	——	——

Chapter 11

Operating MRP II

Imagine the feelings of the winning Super Bowl team. What a kick that must be! They've reached their goal. They're Number One.

Now imagine it's six months later. The team, the coaches, and the team's owner have just held a meeting, and decided to cancel this year's training camp. Their attitude is: "Who needs it? We're the best in the business. We don't have to spend time on fundamentals—things like blocking, tackling and catching footballs. We know how to do that." They've also decided not to hold daily practices during the season. "We'll just go out every Sunday afternoon and do the same things we did last year."

Does this make any sense? Of course not. But, this is exactly the attitude some companies adopt after they become Class A MRP II users. Their approach is: "This MRP II thing's a piece of cake. We don't need to worry about it anymore."

Wrong, of course. George Bevis said it very well: "MRP II is not a destination; it's a journey." No Class A MRP II system will maintain itself. It requires continual attention, constant "care and feeding."

There are two major objectives involved in operating MRP II:

1. Don't let it slip.
2. Make it better and better.

It's easy to let it slip. Some Class A companies have learned this lesson the hard way. They've "taken their eye off the ball," and assumed their MRP II system will maintain itself. In the process, they've lost a letter grade. They've slipped to Class B. (Companies who achieve Class B and make the same mistake can become Class C very quickly.) Then comes the laborious process of reversing the trend and re-acquiring the excellence that once was there. The "flip side" of these experiences is represented by the really excellent MRP II user companies. Their attitude is: "We're Class A, but we're going to do better next year than we did this year. We're not satisfied with the status quo. Our goal is to be even more excellent in the future than we are now." This is what's meant by step 11 on the *Proven Path:* Dedication to Continuing Improvement.

How should a company address these issues? How can they not let it slip? What's involved in making it better and better?

This answer has four key elements:

- Understanding
- Organization
- Measurements
- Education

Let's look at each one.

Understanding

In this context, understanding means lack of arrogance. In the example of the championship football team, things were reversed. They *had* arrogance; they *lacked* understanding. They also lacked any real chance of becoming next year's Super Bowl champions.

Operating at a Class A level is much the same. A company needs to *understand:*

- Today's success is no guarantee of tomorrow's.
- MRP II will not maintain itself; if left unattended, it will deteriorate.
- People are the key.
- The "name of the game" is to win, to be better than the

competition, and operating a Class A MRP II system is the best way to do that.

Organization

Don't disband the MRP II project team and the executive steering committee. Keep these groups going. They're almost as important after a successful implementation as before. However, some changes in the way they operate should be made.

THE MRP II OPERATING COMMITTEE

After implementation is complete, the MRP II project team should remain in place with the following changes:

1. The group now has no full-time members; therefore, it's probably a bit smaller than it was.

2. Since MRP II is no longer a project but rather is operational, the name of the group should be changed to "MRP II operating committee" or something along those lines.

3. Group meetings are held about once a month rather than once a week.

4. The chairmanship of the group rotates among its members, perhaps once or twice a year. First, a marketing manager might be the chairperson, next a manager from accounting, then perhaps someone from engineering or purchasing. This approach enhances the collective sense of "ownership" of MRP II. It states strongly that MRP II is a company-wide system.

The group's job is to focus formally on the performance of the MRP II system, report results to top management, and develop and implement improvements.

SPIN-OFF TASK FORCES

Just as during implementation, these temporary groups can be used to solve specific problems, capitalize on opportunities, etc.

THE EXECUTIVE STEERING COMMITTEE

Following implementation, the executive steering committee should meet about once every six months. It receives updates on MRP II performance from the operating committee. Its tasks are much the same as during implementation: reviewing status, re-allocating resources when necessary, and providing leadership.

Measurements

Manufacturing Resource Planning has two sides: operational and financial. MRP II enables a company to express the operating plan in financial terms. It can "translate" pieces and gallons and standard hours into dollars.

It follows, then, that measuring the effectiveness of MRP II performance requires both operational and financial measurements. Further, operational measurements can be divided into detailed and summary. Let's look at each one.

OPERATIONAL MEASUREMENTS—DETAILED

The purpose of detailed operational measurements is to serve as a continuous check on how MRP II is functioning. It's the early warning system—alerting us when something is starting to go wrong and also helping continually to improve performance.

Listed below is a series of these measurements. This list will probably not be 100% complete for any one company, and further, it contains some elements which may not apply in some organizations. I include it here to serve as a foundation and a point of departure for companies to use in developing their own measurements program.

In production planning, key measurements include sales to forecast, actual production to plan, actual inventory/backlog to plan. Typically, these measurements are monthly, and form the foundation for the production planning meetings.

In master production scheduling, key measurements can include:

1. On-time delivery performance. For make-to-order this means shipping on the date promised; for make-to-stock, it's the order fill rate (orders shipped from stock divided by total orders). For Class A companies, these figures are near 100%.

2. Production performance to the master schedule. The ABCD Checklist calls for 95% minimum.

3. Number of MPS changes in the emergency zone. This should be a very small number.

4. MPS orders rescheduled in compared to those rescheduled out. These numbers should be close to equal.

5. Finished goods inventory turnover, for make-to-stock.

Typically these measurements are done weekly, except for inventory turnover, which is normally a monthly calculation. In material requirements planning, check on:

1. Stock-outs, for both manufactured and purchased items.

2. Inventory turnover, again for both make and buy items.

3. Exception message volume. This refers to the number of action recommendations generated by the MRP program each week. For conventional (fabrication and assembly) manufacturers, the exception rate should be 10% or less. For process and repetitive plants, the rate may be higher due to more activity per part number. (The good news is that these kinds of companies usually have far fewer parts.)

4. Late order releases, the number of orders released with less than the planning lead time remaining. A good target rule of thumb here is 5% or less of all orders released.

5. Shop orders and vendor orders rescheduled in, versus rescheduled out. Here again, these numbers should be close to equal.

Except for inventory turns, most of these measurements are done weekly. Typically they're broken out by planner, including, of course, the vendor schedulers.

In capacity requirements planning, some companies track the past due load. Target: less than one week's work. Frequency: weekly.

In shop floor control, the following are important measurements:

1. On-time shop order completions to the order due date. The ABCD Checklist calls for 95% minimum.

2. On-time shop order completions, to the *operation* due date. A good measurement here is to track late jobs in to a work center compared to late jobs out (completed). This recognizes that a foreman shouldn't be penalized for jobs that arrive behind schedule. Some companies expand this to track "total days of lateness" in and out, rather than merely numbers of jobs. This helps to identify foremen who may be making up some of the lost time even when jobs are completed late.

3. Capacity performance to plan. Standard hours of actual output compared to planned output. A good target: plus or minus 5%.

The frequency of the above: weekly; the breakout: by foremen. Please keep in mind that these are MRP II-related measurements only, and are not intended to replace measures of efficiency, productivity and others.

For purchasing, I recommend measuring stock-outs and inventory turns on purchased material by vendor and by buyer, as well as for the vendor schedulers, as mentioned above. Here also, don't neglect the other important measurements on quality, price, etc. The ABCD Checklist calls for 95% or better vendor delivery performance.

For data, I recommend weekly reports on inventory, bill of material and routing accuracy. The targets for all should be close to 100%.

OPERATIONAL MEASUREMENTS—SUMMARY

The ABCD Checklist, contained in Appendix B, is the essential operational measurement of "how we're doing" operating MRP II.

The ABCD Checklist should be reviewed by the MRP II operating committee formally, as a group, at least twice a year. A consensus, if not unanimity, should be reached on each of the twenty-five questions. For any "No" answer, this group should focus on:

1. What's causing the "No" answer? What's going wrong?

2. What's the best way to fix the problem? Should the company activate a spin-off task force?

3. How quickly can it be fixed? (Set dates—don't let it drift.)

Each time the ABCD Checklist is reviewed, the results are formally communicated to the executive steering committee: the score achieved, the class rating (A,B,C, etc.), what the "No's" are, what's being done about them, and what help if any is needed from top management.

Who does this communication? Who presents these results? The part-time successor to the full-time project leader. In other words, the chairperson of the MRP II operating committee.

FINANCIAL MEASUREMENTS

At least once a year, the MRP II operating committee should take a check on "how we're doing" financially with the system. Actual results, in dollars, should be compared to the benefits projected in the cost justification.

Just as with the operational measurements, a hardnosed and

straightforward approach should be used here: is the company getting at least the benefits expected? If not, why not? Start fixing what's wrong so the company can start to get the bang for the buck. Results are reported to the executive steering committee.

Education

Failure to establish an "airtight" ongoing education program is the single greatest threat to the long-term successful operation of MRP II. See Figure 11-1. Ongoing education is essential because:

- New people enter the company. Plus, current employees move into different jobs within the company, with different and perhaps expanded responsibilities. Failure to educate these new job incumbents spells trouble. It means that, sooner or later, the company will lose that "critical mass" of MRP II-knowledgeable people. The company then will be unable to operate MRP II as effectively as before.

- People tend to forget. They need "refresher" education and training. To borrow a concept from the physical sciences, there's a "half-life" to what one learns. If that half-life is one year, people will remember about half of what they learned about MRP II last year, 25% from two years ago.

- Business conditions change. For any given company, its operating environment three years from now will probably differ substantially from what it is today. Companies develop new product lines, enter new markets, change production processes, become subject to new governmental regulations, acquire new subsidiaries, find that they're operating in a buyers' market (not a sellers' market), or vice versa, and on and on and on.

- Operating MRP II means running the business with that set of tools. The tools within MRP II tend not to change. However, business conditions do change. What's needed period-

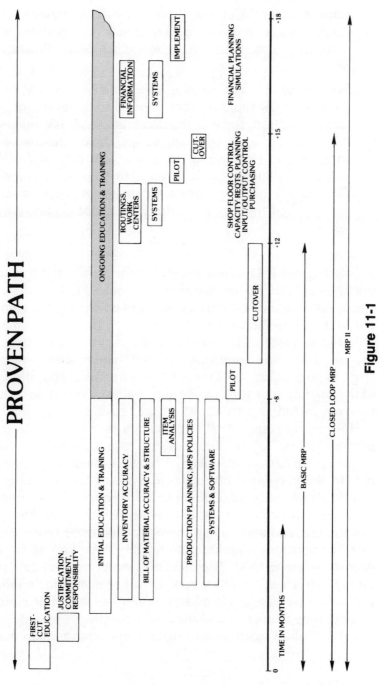

PROVEN PATH

Figure 11-1

ically is to match up the tools (MRP II) to today's business environment and objectives. These may be very different from what they were a few years ago when MRP II was implemented.

What's needed is an ongoing educational process where people can review the tools they're using to do their jobs, match that up against today's requirements, and ask themselves, "Are we still doing the right things? How might we use the tools better? How could we *do our jobs differently* to meet today's challenges?" We're back to behavior change. (See Chapter 6.) It's necessary after implementation, as well as before. And the way to facilitate behavior change is via education.

Ongoing MRP II education should be woven tightly into the operational fabric of the company. Minimum MRP II educational standards should be established for each position in the company, and written into the job specification. New incumbents should be required to meet these standards within the first few weeks on the job. These minimum standards will require some new people to go to outside classes. However, as with initial education, most of the ongoing education can be accomplished via inside education sessions, including virtually all of the refresher education.

How can ongoing MRP II education be "woven into the operational fabric" of the company? Perhaps it can best be done by involving the personnel/industrial relations/human resources people. In the personnel office, there are files for each employee. Checklists are maintained there to help ensure that all employees have signed up for programs like health insurance, the blood drive and the United Fund. Given these files and these types of checklists, the personnel department may be the best group to *administer* the ongoing MRP II educational program, schedule people into classes, track attendance, report and reschedule "no shows," etc. Of course, the inside education sessions would be *conducted* by operating managers and other key people.

Let me add a word about ongoing education for top management. A change in senior management, either at the CEO level or on his staff, is a point of peril for MRP II. If the new executive does not receive the proper education, then he will, in all likelihood, not understand MRP II and may inadvertently cause it to deteriorate. New executives on board need MRP II education more than anyone else. This requirement is absolute and cannot be violated if the company wants to operate MRP II successfully over the long run. Here also, this critically important educational requirement should be built directly into the executive's job specifications as a hard and fast rule, with no latitude permitted.

Maintaining the Software

I cut my teeth in data processing on a GE-415 computer. General Electric doesn't make computers anymore. A friend of mine used to own a data processing service bureau, where they used RCA Spectra 70s. RCA doesn't make computers anymore. A high percentage of the Class A companies still use the old IBM PICS package (almost without exception heavily modified and enhanced). IBM doesn't support PICS any longer.

The message is clear. My colleague, Chris Gray, says it very well: "Prepare for the day when you will have to maintain the MRP II software yourself." Don't assume the software supplier will maintain the package forever. They may not even be in business five years from now.

Assume the day will come when the software vendor will no longer support the package. Personally, I'd choose to assume that day will come sooner, rather than later. If possible, I'd maintain it myself right from the start. If not, I'd take it over just as soon as I could.

Remember: software is a set of tools which will become *essential* to how the business is run. Is it wise to be heavily dependent on an outside source for the maintenance of that critically important resource?

Beyond Class A—The Launch Pad to Total Excellence

"How are we doing?" is one necessary question to ask routinely. Another is "How can we do it better?"

Don't neglect this second question. The really excellent MRP II-using companies seem to share a discontent with the status quo. Their attitude is: "We're doing great, but we're going to be even better next year. We're going to raise the high bar another six inches, and go for it."

There are few companies today who are as good as they could be. There are few companies today who even have any idea how good they could be. In general, the really excellent MRP II-using companies are populated with individuals no smarter or harder working than elsewhere. They merely "got there" first, then stayed there (at Class A), and then got better and better.

With a Class A MRP II system, a company can operate at an excellent level of performance—far better than before, probably better than it ever dreamed possible. In this context, Class A MRP II can be considered as an end in itself.

Are all Class A companies perfect? Nope. Are there things that Class A companies could do better? Darn right, and that's the place for the superb tools like CAD/CAM, Just-In-Time, Group Technology, Computer Integrated Manufacturing, Statistical Process Control, and the others mentioned back in Chapter 1.

The message is clear. Companies should not rest on their laurels after reaching Class A. Don't be content with the status quo. It's more important than ever to go after those additional productivity tools, those "better mousetraps," those better and more humane ways of dealing with people. Many of these projects can be funded with the cash freed up by the inventory reductions made possible by MRP II. Look upon your Class A system as an engine, a vehicle, a launch pad for total excellence. Without that attitude, you'll never know how good you can be. You'll never know where the outer limits are.

Good luck and Godspeed.

IMPLEMENTERS' CHECKLIST

Function: OPERATING MRP II

Task	Complete Yes	No
1. MRP II project team reorganized for ongoing operation, with no full-time members and rotating chairmanship.	____	____
2. Executive steering committee still in place.	____	____
3. ABCD Checklist and financial measurements generated by project team twice per year and formally reported to executive steering committee.	____	____
4. Ongoing MRP II education program underway and woven into the operational fabric of the company.	____	____
5. Discontent with the status quo and dedication to continuing improvement adopted as a way of life within the company.	____	____

Appendices A, B and C are taken from *Manufacturing Resource Planning: MRP II—Unlocking America's Productivity Potential* by Oliver Wight, Oliver Wight Limited Publications, Inc., 1981.

The Mechanics of Manufacturing Resource Planning (MRP II)

Section 1
The Closed Loop System

The logic of the closed loop MRP system is extremely simple. It's in every cookbook. The "bill of material" says, "Turkey stuffing takes one egg, seasoning, bread crumbs, etc." The routing says, "Put the egg and the seasoning in a blender." The blender is the work center. The master schedule is Thanksgiving.

But, in manufacturing, there is a lot more volume and a lot more change. There isn't just one product. There are many. The lead times aren't as short as going to the corner store. The work centers are busy rather than waiting for work—because some of them cost a third of a million dollars or more—and it simply is not wise economically to let them sit idle and to have excess capacity. In addition, the sales department will undoubtedly change the date of Thanksgiving several times before it actually arrives! And this isn't through perversity. This is because the customers want and need some things earlier or later.

The volume of activity in manufacturing is monumentally high; something is happening all the time. And change is the norm, not the exception.

But the point is that the *logic* of MRP is very straightforward indeed. Figure A-1 shows the closed loop system.

The production plan is the *rate* of production for a product family typically expressed in units like, "We want to produce 1100 Model 30 pumps per week." The production plan is made by taking into account current inventory, deciding whether inventory needs to go up or down during the planning period, projecting the sales forecast, and determining the rate of production required to maintain, raise, or lower the inventory level. For a make-to-order product, as opposed to a make-to-stock product, the "order backlog" rather than the inventory is the starting point for the production plan.

Figure A-2 shows a typical production plan. Figure A-3 shows a business plan which is simply an extension of the production plan into dollars. The complete business plan in a manufacturing company will include research and development and other expenses not directly related to production and purchases. But the core of any business plan in a manufacturing enterprise is the production plan. With MRP II, the production plan and business plan are interdependent and, as the production plan is updated, it is extended into dollars to show it in the common denominator of business—money.

The closed loop MRP system then takes a master schedule ("What are we going to make?"), "explodes" this through the bill of material ("What does it take to make it?"), and compares

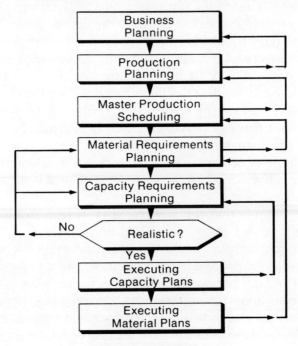

Figure A-1 MRP II

Month Ending		Sales (thousands)	Production (thousands)	Inventory (thousands)
3/31	Plan			
	Actual			60
4/30	Plan	30	35	65
	Actual	25	36	71
6/30	Plan	30	35	75
	Actual			

Figure A-2 Production Plan

this with the inventory on hand and on order ("What do we have?") to determine material requirements ("What do we have to get?").

This fundamental material requirements planning logic is shown in Figure A-4. Figure A-5 shows the bill of material. For this example, a small gasoline engine for a moped is the product being manufactured. The bill of material shown in Figure A-5 is what's known as an "indented bill of material." This simply means that the highest level items in the bill of material are shown farthest left. For example, the piston assembly components are "indented" to the right to indicate that they go into that assembly. Therefore, in this example, they are at "level 2."

A bill of material "in reverse" is called a "where-used" list. It would say, for example, that the locating pins go into the crankcase half-left, which goes into the engine.

Month Ending		Sales (thousands)	Production (thousands)	Inventory (thousands)
3/31	Plan			
	Actual			6,000
4/30	Plan	3,000	3,500	6,500
	Actual	2,500	3,600	7,100
5/31	Plan	3,000	3,500	7,000
	Actual	3,800	3,200	6,500
6/30	Plan	3,000	3,500	7,500
	Actual	3,200	3,700	7,000
12/31	Plan	3,000	3,500	10,500
	Actual			

Figure A-3 Business Plan

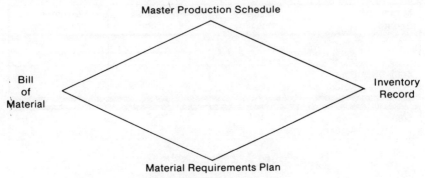

Figure A-4 MRP Logic

Part Number	
87502	Cylinder Head
94411	Crankshaft
94097	Piston Assembly
91776	Piston
84340	Wristpin
81111	Connecting Rod—Top Half
27418	Connecting Rod—Bottom Half
81743	Piston Rings Compression (2)
96652	Piston Ring Oil
20418	Bearing Halves (2)
59263	Lock Bolts (2)
43304	Crankcase Half Right
28079	Crankcase Half Left
80021	Locater Pins (2)

Figure A-5 Moped Engine Bill of Material

Master Production Schedule
Engines

	Week							
	1	2	3	4	5	6	7	8
Master Schedule	80	0	100	0	0	120	0	120
Actual Demand	40	40	30	30	30	40	40	20
Available to Promise	0	0	10	0	0	40	0	100

Figure A-6 Master Production Schedule

Figure A-6 shows a master schedule for engines. In a make-to-stock company, the master schedule would be very similar, but it would take into account the inventory on hand.

Section 2
Material Requirements Planning

Figure A-7 shows the material requirements plan for the crankcase half-left and also for the locator pin that goes into the crankcase half-left. The projected gross requirements come from the master schedule plus any service parts requirements. "Scheduled receipts" are the orders that are already in production or out with the vendors. The projected available balance takes the on-hand figure, subtracts requirements from it, and adds scheduled re-

Material Requirements Plan
Crankcase Half — Left

LEAD TIME = 4 WEEKS ORDER QUANTITY = 200		Week							
		1	2	3	4	5	6	7	8
Projected Gross Requirements		80	0	100	0	0	120	0	120
Scheduled Receipts				240					
Proj. Avail. Bal.	120	40	40	180	180	180	60	60	-60
Planned Order Release					200				

Material Requirements Plan
Locater Pin (2 Per)

LEAD TIME = 4 WEEKS ORDER QUANTITY = 500		Week							
		1	2	3	4	5	6	7	8
Projected Gross Requirements					400				400*
Scheduled Receipts									-
Proj. Avail. Bal.	430	430	430	430	30	30	30	30	-370
Planned Order Release					500				

*Requirements from Another Crankcase

Figure A-7 Material Requirements Plan

ceipts to it. (In Figure A-7, the starting on-hand balance is 120 for the crankcase half-left.) This calculation projects future inventory balances to indicate when material needs to be ordered or rescheduled.

The material on hand and on order subtracted from the gross requirements yields "net requirements" (60 in week 8 for the crankcase half-left in Figure A-8). This is the amount that is actually needed to cover requirements. When the net requirements are converted to lot sizes and backed off over the lead time, they are called "planned order releases."

The "planned order releases" at one level in the product structure—in this case 200 "crankcase half-left"—become the projected gross requirements at the lower level. The 200-unit planned order release in period four for the crankcase half-left becomes a projected gross requirement of 400 locater pins in period four since there are two locater pins per crankcase half-left.

MRP — Rescheduling
Crankcase Half — Left

LEAD TIME = 4 WEEKS ORDER QUANTITY = 200	Week							
	1	2	3	4	5	6	7	8
Projected Gross Requirements		80	0	100	0	0	120	0	120
Scheduled Receipts					240				
Proj. Avail. Bal.	120	40	40	-60	180	180	60	60	-60
Planned Order Release					200				

MRP — Locater Pin (2 Per)

LEAD TIME = 4 WEEKS ORDER QUANTITY = 500	Week							
	1	2	3	4	5	6	7	8
Projected Gross Requirements					400				400*
Scheduled Receipts									
Proj. Avail. Bal.	430	430	430	430	30	30	30	30	-370
Planned Order Release					500				

*Requirements from Another Crankcase

Figure A-8 MRP—Rescheduling

Most MRP systems also include what is called "pegged requirements." This is simply a way to trace where the requirements came from. For example, the pegged requirements for the locater pins would indicate that the 400 in period four came from the crankcase half-left and that the 400 in period eight came from another product. Pegged requirements show the quantity, the time period, and the higher level item where the requirements are coming from.

Figure A-8 shows the same crankcase half as in Figure A-7. Note, however, that now the scheduled receipt is shown in period four. This means that the due date on the shop order or the purchase order is week four. An MRP system would generate a reschedule message for the planner to move the scheduled receipt from week four into week three to cover the requirements in week three.

Note, also, that the fact that the scheduled receipt for the crankcase half needs to be rescheduled does not affect the requirements for locater pins. The locater pins have already been released into production for the crankcase halves that are on order. The "requirements" for locater pins are for planned orders that have *not* been released yet.

The bill of material is the instrument for converting planned order releases at one level into projected gross requirements at a lower level. The bill of material for the crankcase half-left, for example, would show that two locater pins per crankcase half were required.

Section 3
Capacity Planning and Scheduling

Capacity planning for the manufacturing facility follows the same general logic as the material requirements planning shown in Figure A-4. Figure A-9 shows this capacity requirements planning logic. The remaining operations on released shop orders and all of the operations on planned order releases are "exploded" through the routings (like bills of material for operations) and posted against the work centers (like an inventory of capacities). The result is a capacity requirements plan in standard hours by work center showing the number of standard hours required to meet the material requirements plan. This capacity requirements plan shows the capacity that will be required to execute the master schedule, and consequently, the production plan.

It's important to note that everything in a closed loop MRP system is in "lock step." If the capacity to meet the material requirements plan can't be obtained either through a company's own manufacturing facilities, subcontracting, or purchasing material on the outside, obviously the master schedule will have to be changed. But that is the last resort. The objective is to make the master schedule happen.

Operations scheduling involves assigning individual schedule dates to the operations on a shop order using scheduling rules. Scheduling rules would typically be similar to these:

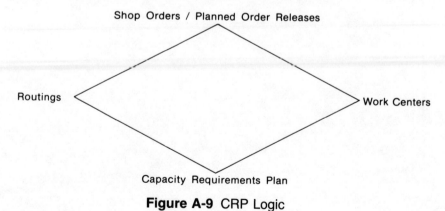

Figure A-9 CRP Logic

1. Allow two days for inspection. (This is a matter of judgment.)

2. Round the standard hours up to the nearest day.

3. Allow X days for queue time.

4. Release work to stockroom one week prior to first operation.

Scheduling with a regular calendar is extremely awkward. For example, if a job was to be completed on August 31 (see Figure A-10) and the last operation—inspection—was scheduled to take two days, the previous operation would have to be completed on August 27, not August 29 (Sunday) or August 28 (Saturday). The scheduler would have to reference the calendar continuously to avoid scheduling work on weekends, holidays, during plant vacation shutdown week, etc. Figure A-11 shows a "shop calendar" where only the working days are numbered. This allows the scheduler to do simple arithemetic like "subtract two days from day 412," thus the previous operation is to be completed on day 410.

Calendar						
AUGUST						
S	M	T	W	T	F	S
1	2	3	4	5	6	7
8	9	10	11	12	13	14
15	16	17	18	19	20	21
22	23	24	25	26	27	28
29	30	31				

Figure A-10 Calendar

Calendar						
AUGUST						
S	M	T	W	T	F	S
1	2 391	3 392	4 393	5 394	6 395	7
8	9 396	10 397	11 398	12 399	13 400	14
15	16 401	17 402	18 403	19 404	20 405	21
22	23 406	24 407	25 408	26 409	27 410	28
29	30 411	31 412				

Figure A-11 Calendar

Shop calendars are in very common use in manufacturing companies today, but they do have drawbacks. People don't relate to these calendars as easily as they do to a regular calendar. And, of course, they are awkward in dealing with customers who don't use the same shop calendar. Therefore, the shop calendar dates must, once again, be translated back to regular calendar dates. There is a simple solution to this problem with today's computers. A shop calendar can be put in the computer and the computer can do the scheduling using the shop calendar, but print the schedule dates out in regular calendar days. If a company has a shop calendar, there is no reason to discontinue using it if people are used to it. On the other hand, there is no need to introduce the shop calendar today when the computer can do the conversion.

Figure A-12 shows a shop order for the locater pin. This will be used as an example of operations scheduling and, in this example, a shop calendar *will* be used in order to make the arithmetic of scheduling clear. The due date is day 412 and that is determined, in the case of the locater pin that goes into the crankcase half-left, from the material requirements plan.

Operations scheduling works back from this need date to put scheduled finish dates on each operation using scheduling rules like those discussed above. Inspection will be allowed two days. Thus, finish turn must be completed on day 410. It is assumed that the work center file indicates that there are two shifts working in work center 1204 (two shifts at 8 hours apiece equals 16 hours), thus the 27.3 hours required for finish turn will take two days. Planned queue time in this example is assumed to be two days ahead of finish turn. Rough turn must be completed four days earlier than the finish turn must be completed, and its scheduled finish date, therefore, is day 406. The standard hours are calculated by multiplying the quantity by the time per piece and, in this case, adding in the setup time. Where machine operators do not set up their own machines, it might make sense to keep this separate.

It is important to recognize that Figure A-12 shows the information that would be in the computer. *The finish dates would not appear on the shop paperwork that was released to the factory.* The reason is that material requirements planning would be constantly reviewing the need date to see if it had changed. If, for example, the left crankcase halves are scrapped because of a problem with the castings, and the best possible date to have a new lot of castings for the crankcase halves is day 422, the master

Shop Order NN. 18447
Part No. 80021 — Locater Pin
Quant. 500   Due: 412   Release 395

Oper.	Dept.	Work Center	Desc.	Setup	Per Piece	Std. Hrs.	Finish
10	08	1322	Cut Off	.5	.010	5.5	402
20	32	1600	Rough Turn	1.5	.030	16.5	406
30	32	1204	Finish Turn	3.3	.048	27.3	410
40	11		Inspect				412

Figure A-12 Shop Order NN. 18447

schedule would be changed to indicate that. The shop order for the locater pins in the computer would be given a new finish date of 422 and operation 30 would then become 420, operation 20 would become 416, etc.

Capacity requirements will not be posted against the work centers using the routine shown in Figure A-9. A capacity plan, as shown in Figure A-13, will be the result.

This capacity plan has, of course, been cut apart to show it in the figure. It would include many more shop orders, as well as the planned order releases from MRP, in reality. The locater pins are shown here as a released shop order. (Note: there is no released shop order for locater pins in Figure A-8. It would show as a "scheduled receipt" if there were.) One of the great values of MRP is the fact that it projects "planned order releases." These planned order releases are used to:

1. Generate lower level material requirements.

2. Generate capacity requirements.

3. Determine when lower level material—both purchased and manufactured—must be rescheduled to earlier or later dates.

This ability to see capacity requirements ahead of time is especially important to good manpower planning. Seeing the capacity requirements coming rather than seeing the backlogs of

			Work Center	1600			
Part No.	SO No.	Qty.	Week 396- 400	Week 401- 405	Week 406- 410	Week 411- 415	Week 416- 420
91762	17621	50		3.5			
80021	18447	500			16.5		
Includes Planned Orders							
Total Std. Hrs.			294	201	345	210	286

Figure A-13 Capacity Requirements Plan

work out on the factory floor enables factory supervision to do a far better job of leveling production, resulting in less overtime, and less need to hire and lay off people on a short-term basis.

Figure A-14 shows a summary of the capacity requirements over an eight-week period. In practice, this would typically be projected over a far longer period. The summary is drawn from the capacity requirements plan illustrated in Figure A-13 which would also extend much further into the future than the five weeks shown. A typical manpower plan would extend three to six months into the future and would be calculated weekly. A "facilities plan" that would be used for determining what new machine tools were needed would be calculated typically once every two to three months and extended three to four years into the future because of the lead time for procuring machine tools.

The most important information for a foreman is the average hours that he must plan to turn out. This production rate is usually calculated as a four-week average because the individual weekly hours are not particularly significant. The variations between these hours are more random than real. Figure A-13 shows one reason why this happens. The 16.5 hours for part number 80021, the locator pin, are shown in the week bracketed by days 406 to 410. Referring back to Figure A-12, it can be seen that these 16.5 hours are *actually going to be in work center 1600 Tuesday of the previous week!*

Many people have tried to develop elaborate computer load

**Capacity Requirements
Summary (in Standard Hours)**

Week	4-Week Total	4-Week Average	Hours	Week	4-Week Total	4-Week Average	Hours
1	294			5	286		
2	201			6	250		
3	345			7	315		
4	210	1050	263	8	257	1108	277

Figure A-14 Capacity Requirements Summary (in Standard Hours)

leveling systems because they were alarmed by the weekly variation in the apparent "load" shown in the capacity requirements plan. These variations are random. They are exaggerated by the fact that capacity plans are usually done in weekly time periods, and any foreman can attest to the fact that the hours never materialize exactly the same way they are shown on the plan. The most important thing to know is the average rate of output required so that *manpower* can be planned accordingly.

In Figure A-14, the four-week averages are 263 standard hours for the first four weeks and 277 for the second four weeks, or an average of 270 standard hours per week. Now the capacity planner must determine whether that capacity requirement can be met. The first step is to find out what the output from the work center has been over the last few weeks. This is called "demonstrated capacity." (This term was coined by David Garwood and is very useful in describing the present capacity of a work center as opposed to its potential capacity when all shifts are manned, etc.)

It is the job of the capacity planner to then determine whether or not the current capacity is sufficient. Or, what needs to be done to get the capacity to meet the plan. Or—as a last resort—to feed back information that the plan cannot be met.

If the plan cannot be met, the master schedule and, perhaps, even the production plans will have to be changed. If, for example, a company has one broach and it is the only one of its type available because it was made specifically for this company, it could well become a bottleneck. If the capacity plan indicates that more hours were required at the broach than could possibly be produced, the master schedule would have to be changed to reflect this.

Once again, however, it's important to emphasize that this is the *last resort*. The job of the capacity planner is to get the capacity that is needed to meet the plan. And that is an important point to emphasize. If there is any problem that exists in practice with capacity planning, it is the fact that people expect the computer to do the capacity planning rather than recognizing that all it can do is generate numbers that will be given to an intelligent, experienced person—the capacity planner—to use in working with other people to fix capacity problems.

Once it is agreed that the capacity requirements can be met, an output control report as shown in Figure A-15 is set up. Three weeks have passed since the one in the figure was made, and the actual standard hours produced (shown in the second line of the figure) are falling far short of the required standard hours at work center 1600. The deviation in the first week was 20 hours. In the second week, it was 50 hours—for a cumulative deviation of 70 hours. In the third week, it was 80 hours, giving a total cumulative deviation of 150 hours. This is a true *control* report with a plan and feedback to show where actual output in standard hours compares with the plan. It shows the deviation from the plan. The 150 hour deviation in week three indicates that 150 standard hours of work required to produce material to meet the master schedule has not been completed.

The amount of tolerance around the plan has to be established. If it were determined, for example, that the company could tolerate being one half week behind schedule, the tolerance in Figure A-15 would be 135 standard hours. When the deviation exceeds 135 standard hours, that would require immediate attention to increase output through overtime, adding people, etc. Whenever the planned rate in the output control report is changed, the deviation will be reset to 0.

It's a good idea to show input to a work center as well as output. That way, when a work center is behind on output because a feeding work center has not given them the work, it can be de-

Output Control
Work Center 1600
Week No. 4
(in Std. Hrs.)

Today

	Week 1	Week 2	Week 3	Week 4
Planned	270	270	270	270
Actual Std.	250	220	190	
Deviation	–20	–70	–150	

Figure A-15 Output Control

tected very quickly since the input report will show the actual input below the planned input. This is called an "input/output report."

The capacity planning and output control reports are concerned with capacity. The dispatch list shown in Figure A-16 is concerned with priority.

The dispatch list is generated daily—or as required—and goes out to the shop floor at the beginning of the day. It shows the sequence in which the jobs are to be run according to the scheduled date for the operation in that work center. The movement of jobs from work center to work center is put in to the computer so that each morning the foremen can have an up-to-date schedule that is driven by MRP. If part 80021 had been rescheduled to a new completion date of day 422 as discussed above, its priority would drop on the dispatch list because its scheduled date would now be 416. This would allow part number 44318 to be made earlier. The dispatch list gives the foremen the priority of jobs so that they can pick the proper job to start next. Since the dispatch list is driven by MRP, it tells the foremen the right sequence in which to run the jobs to do the best job of preventing predicted shortages.

Dispatch List Work Center No. 1600				Day 405
Shop Order No.	Part No.	Qty.	Scheduled Date	Std. Hours
17621	91762	50	401	3.5
18430	98340	500	405	19.2
18707	78212	1100	405	28.6
18447	80021	500	406	16.5
19712	44318	120	409	8.4
			Total Hours	76.2

Figure A-16 Dispatch List

Section 4
The MRP Output Reports

The figures in this chapter represent the major reports that are used in a closed loop MRP system. Referring back to Figure A-1, the functions of the production plan (Figure A-2), the master schedule (Figure A-6), the material requirements plan (Figures A-7 and A-8), and the capacity requirements plan (Figure A-13) are illustrated. The output control report (Figure A-15) is the means for monitoring output against the plan to be sure that capacity plans are being executed. The dispatch list (Figure A-16) is the report for the factory to use in executing the material plans. Vendor scheduling is the way the material requirements plans are executed with the "outside factories."

It is important to emphasize the feedback functions in a closed loop system. For example, if vendors are not going to ship on time, they must send in an anticipated delay report as soon as they recognize that they have a problem. In the past, ship dates were not valid. The typical company had many past due purchase orders with the vendor. With MRP—if it is properly managed—dates will represent real need dates, and, thus, it is important to feed back information as quickly as possible to indicate when these dates cannot be met. This, of course, is also true for the factory, where the anticipated delay report should be a regular part of their feedback to the closed loop system.

A closed loop MRP system is a fairly modern development. Many companies talked about material requirements planning for years and *did* explode bills of material on a computer. But, it was the advent of the modern computer with its great processing speeds and storage capabilities that made modern MRP practical. The ability to break requirements down into weekly, or even daily, time periods rather than showing them in monthly increments, for example, helped MRP to become a scheduling system rather than just another order launching system (even though it is superior to the order point as an ordering system). The ability to plan requirements weekly—or even daily—made MRP a practical scheduling tool. Before 1971, it would be hard to find any closed loop MRP system in existence. Master scheduling was not well understood. Capacity planning and dispatching were tried, but were usually ineffective because the priority planning wasn't valid. Computers of the day couldn't keep schedules up-to-date and the people using them didn't understand how to master schedule properly to do this. Closed loop MRP is truly a product of the computer age.

ABCD Checklist

The ABCD Checklist is for companies that are currently *operating* MRP systems and want to measure their effectiveness.

A *Class A* MRP user is one that uses MRP in a closed loop mode. They have material requirements planning, capacity planning and control, shop floor dispatching, and vendor scheduling systems in place and being used.

And management uses the system to run the business. They participate in production planning. They sign off on the production plans. They constantly monitor performance on inventory record accuracy, bill of material accuracy, routing accuracy, attainment of the master schedule, attainment of the capacity plans, etc.

In a Class A company, the MRP system provides the game plan that sales, finance, manufacturing, purchasing, and engineering people all work to. They *use* the formal system. The foremen and the purchasing people work to the schedules. There is no shortage list to override the schedules and answer the question, "What material is really needed when?"—that answer comes from the formal MRP system.

Companies using MRP II have gone even a step beyond Class A. They have tied in the financial system and developed simulation capabilities so that the "what if" questions can be answered using the system. In this type of company, management can work with one set of numbers to run the business because the operating system and the financial system use the same numbers.

Technically, then, an MRP II system has the financial and operating systems married together and has a simulation capability. But, the important point is that the system is used as a company game plan. This is what really makes a company Class A.

A *Class B* company has material requirements planning and usually capacity requirements planning and shop floor control systems in place. The Class B user typically hasn't done much with purchasing yet and differs from the Class A user primarily because top management doesn't really use the system to run the business directly. Instead, Class B users see MRP as a production and inventory control system. Because of this, it's easy for a Class B user to become a Class C user very quickly. Another characteristic of the Class B company is that they do *some* scheduling in the shop using MRP, but their shortage list is what really tells them what to make. Class B users typically see most of their benefits from MRP in inventory reduction and improved customer service because they do have more of the right things going through production. Because they haven't succeeded in getting the expediting "monkey" off the backs of the purchasing people and foremen, they haven't seen substantial benefits in reduced purchase costs or improved productivity—and they still have more inventory than they really need.

A *Class C* company uses MRP primarily as an inventory ordering technique rather than as a scheduling technique. Shop scheduling is still being done from the shortage list, and the master schedule in a Class C company is typically overstated. They have not really closed the loop. They probably will get some benefits in inventory reduction as a result of MRP.

A *Class D* company only has MRP really working in the data processing department. Typically, their inventory records are poor. If they have a defined master schedule, it's usually grossly overstated and mismanaged, and little or no results have come from the installation of the MRP system. Ironically, except for the education costs, a Class D company will have spent almost as much as a Class A company. They will have spent about 80% of the total, but not achieved the results.

HOW TO USE THE CHECKLIST

Go through the checklist, and try to honestly evaluate where your company stands. This should involve at least two or three people, and there are some instances where partial credit would be ap-

The ABCD Checklist

	YES	NO

Technical

1. Time periods for master production scheduling and Material Requirements Planning are weeks or smaller.
2. Master production scheduling and Material Requirements Planning run weekly or more frequently.
3. System includes firm planned order and pegging capability.
4. The master production schedule is visibly managed, not automatic.
5. System includes capacity requirements planning.
6. System includes daily dispatch list.
7. System included input/output control.

Data Integrity

8. Inventory record accuracy 95% or better.
9. Bill of material accuracy 98% or better.
10. Routing accuracy 95% or better.

Education

11. Initial education of at least 80% of all employees.
12. An ongoing education program.

Use of the System

13. The shortage list has been eliminated.
14. Vendor delivery performance is 95% or better.
15. Vendor scheduling is done out beyond the quoted lead times.
16. Shop delivery performance is 95% or better.
17. Master schedule performance is 95% or better.
18. There are regular (at least monthly) production planning meetings with the general manager and his staff including manufacturing, production and inventory control, engineering, marketing, finance.
19. There is a written master scheduling policy which is adhered to.
20. The system is used for scheduling as well as ordering.
21. MRP is well understood by key people in manufacturing, marketing, engineering, finance, and top management.
22. Management really uses MRP to manage.
23. Engineering changes are effectively implemented.
24. Simultaneous improvement has been achieved in at least two of the following three areas: inventory, productivity, customer service.
25. Operating system is used for financial planning.

propriate. Question 3, for example, could have half credit (two points since the questions each rate four points). Question 21 is another one that could generate partial credit.

A Class A user would be one where the company rated 90 points or higher on the checklist. From 70 to 90 makes a company a Class B user; from 50 to 70, a Class C user; and below 50, a Class D user.

Each company has to use this as a guide in evaluating themselves. If, for example, a company doesn't have any real manufacturing, but only purchases and assembles, then questions 5 and 6 would not apply, and full credit would be given even through the company doesn't have capacity planning and a daily dispatch list.

When the weakest areas in the company are identified, then the important issue is to fix the problems. And the problems always come back to people, and their understanding at one level or another. For example, if inventory record accuracy isn't good, that may be because the stockroom people don't understand. It may be because their supervisor doesn't understand, or it may be because the plant manager to whom the stockroom reports doesn't hold people accountable for inventory record accuracy because the plant manager doesn't understand. Understanding is a case of education, and management conveying a message to people about running a business more professionally.

The Implementation Plan

MRP II DETAILED IMPLEMENTATION PLAN

More and more people are asking for information on the implementation and operation of MRP systems. These people are not interested in being sold on MRP. MRP systems work. The proof is available and companies are using them every day. People who understand the fundamentals and the logical simplicity of MRP are looking for a proven way to implement the system.

This detailed implementation plan is a road map to help people implement MRP systems. The implementation plan outlines the basic functional areas needed to implement MRP. These functional areas are then broken down into specific milestones. This listing of broad functional areas and specific tasks provides a very practical plan.

PEOPLE USING MRP

The implementation plan is also meant for companies using an MRP system. There are many companies which have the technical part of an MRP system in place. Yet, they are not using the system well. The implementation plan can help these companies. The jobs in improving an MRP system are the same as the jobs to implement it correctly. The only difference is that some of these jobs may have already been done. If so, they can be deleted from the plan.

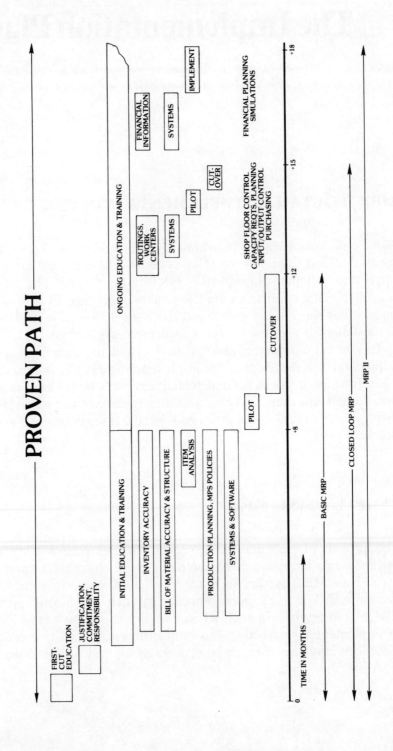

USING THE PLAN

The implementation plan is a generalized framework applicable to nearly any company. Its two primary uses are:

1. To provide a clear statement of priorities—to separate the vital and trivial, and keep them in perspective.

2. To provide a road map for implementation.

The implementation plan is organized to constantly focus attention on the items that have the greatest impact on the potential for success. The people part of an MRP system is fully 80% of the system. The system will only work when people understand what it is, how it works, and what their responsibilities are. For this reason, the education and training are listed at the front of the implementation plan. The computer software and programming effort is not as likely to be something which prevents the success of an MRP system, and so this topic is covered later in the plan.

The other purpose is to provide a detailed schedule of events that have to be accomplished in order to implement the system. The most effective way to use the plan is to tailor the plan to each company and then use it as the agenda for management reviews of implementation progress.

PRACTICALITY

This implementation plan is not a theoretical exercise. In the six years since the first version of the plan was developed, it has been used successfully by a number of companies. Whether these companies would have been successful without the plan, I cannot say. But it does work, it is practical, and those who have used it swear by it.

TAILORING THE PLAN TO YOUR COMPANY

The implementation plan is a general framework stated in terms of departments and job titles. The departments and job titles should be replaced by the names of the people within the organization who will be responsible for the tasks.

The implementation plan also contains an approximate time frame for scheduling the tasks under each of the functional topics. The scheduled due dates for the tasks in implementation are given under the heading "DATE." These due dates were developed based on the dependence of some tasks on others. The times on the plan, +3 and +7 for example, are months relative to a starting point. A time of +3 means the task should be completed three months after the start date. The start date used in the plan is the date that formal commitment is given to the project.

The plan should be rewritten to include calendar dates in place of the scheduled completion dates in months. Columns should also be added for the scheduled start date, the actual start date, and the actual completion date. The scheduled start dates are not on the generalized plan since the size of the different tasks will vary from company to company. The actual start and actual completion dates should be included on the plan to indicate the progress or lack of it during the management reviews of implementation.

The comments column on the implementation plan is meant to give a short explanation of the phases of the plan and tasks that make up each phase. Some people choose to leave these explanations in the final version of the plan, others leave them out. In either case, additional comments on the progress of the tasks should also be included as the plan is periodically updated. These comments would indicate, for example, the results of the cycle counts, or any other information about one of the items in the plan.

A company may also have to add or delete tasks from the implementation plan to account for situations that are a part of the implementation, or work that has already been done. As an example of an item that would be deleted from the plan, a company may have already enclosed the stockrooms and may have started cycle counting. In this case, it makes no sense to count 100 parts as a starting point. As an example of an item that would have to be added to the plan, a company may have to convert to a different computer to do MRP. In this case, the conversion from one computer to the other should be included on the detailed implementation plan.

Figure C-1 is an example of the implementation plan before and after it has been tailored to a company. This example includes replacement of departments and job titles with people's names, the inclusion of calendar dates with columns for scheduling dates, and some comments on tasks that are working.

MRP DETAILED IMPLEMENTATION PLAN

TASK	RESPONSIBLE	DATE	COMMENTS
A. Measure 100 parts as a starting point.	Stockroom Mgr.	+1	This will help assess the work that needs to be done to bring the inventory records to 95%.
B. Map out limited access to the stockroom areas.	Stockroom Mgr.	+1	Lay out any stockroom changes that are necessary to insure limited access.
C. Provide the tools for limited access and transaction recording.	Top Management Stockroom Mgr. Team Leader DP Mgr.	+3	A fence, enough stockroom people, adequate space, counting scales, transaction forms, labels, skids, etc.

TASK	RESPONSIBLE	— SCHEDULED — START	DUE	— ACTUAL — START	DUE
A. Measure 100 parts as a starting point.	R. Ferris	6/20/80	6/27/80	6/20/80	6/24/80
		Results indicate that the inventory accuracy is 63%.			
B. Map out limited access to the stockroom areas.	R. Ferris K. Miller	6/1/80	7/1/80	6/5/80	
		Lay out any stockroom changes that are necessary to insure limited access. Main and spare parts stockrooms to be enclosed and third stockroom to be consolidated into the existing stockrooms.			
C. Provide the tools for limited access and transaction recording.	D. Roser R. Ferris K. Miller H. Arner	7/15/80	9/1/80		
		A fence, enough stockroom people, adequate space, counting scales, transaction forms, labels, skids, etc.			

Figure C-1

MRP DETAILED IMPLEMENTATION PLAN

TASK	RESPONSIBLE	DATE	COMMENTS
1. First-cut education.	Top Management P&IC Shop Management	−1	What is MRP and how does it work? Why should we, as a company, commit to it? The courses should be the equivalent of the following courses offered by The Oliver Wight Companies P.O. Box 435 Newbury, New Hampshire 03255 (800) 258-3862 or (603) 763-5926
	Top Management P&IC Shop Management		MRP II: Manufacturing Resource Planning For Top Management MRP II: Manufacturing Resource Planning - 5 Day
2. Justification, commitment, and assignment of responsibility.	Top Management P&IC	0	Formal commitment to the project.
A. Prepare justification.	P&IC Shop Management	0	Cost/Benefit.
B. Commit to the project.	Top Management	0	
C. Set up implementation team and team leader.	Top Management	0	Implementation team leader is full-time. His responsibility is to make the MRP system work by coordinating and managing the project.
D. Schedule periodic management project reviews.	Top Management	0	Approximately every month. To include all those responsible for parts of the project currently active.
E. Schedule periodic visits from a consultant with experience in implementing successful MRP systems.	Top Management	0	The consultant should have successfully implemented a system or worked with successful systems. Schedule visits from once a month to once every three months.

MRP DETAILED IMPLEMENTATION PLAN

TASK	RESPONSIBLE	DATE	COMMENTS
3. **Detailed education and training.**	Team Leader	0+8	This phase of the plan is aimed at the people part of the system.
			The objective of this part of the plan is to give the people operating the system an understanding of the system and the means to use it effectively. Education and training must translate the general principles of MRP into the specifics of operation at the company.
			The plan separates education and training. Education is the broad-based understanding of MRP which is essential. Training is the detailed knowledge of reports, forms, etc.
			The education and training are structured in levels. People in the company attend outside courses. These people then serve as teachers and train their own people.
A. Outside courses for people who will be teachers at the in-house courses.	Team Leader	+1+3	The courses should be the equivalent of the following courses offered by The Oliver Wight Companies P. O. Box 435 Newbury, New Hampshire 03255 (800) 258-3862 or (603) 763-5926
	Steering Committee Chairman		MRP II: Manufacturing Resource Planning—5-Day
	P&IC Mgr.		MRP II: Successful Implementation
	Purch. Mgr.		MRP II: Successful Implementation
	Plant Supt.		MRP II: Manufacturing Resource Planning—5-Day
	Stockroom Mgr.		MRP II: Manufacturing Resource Planning—5-Day
	Engr. Mgr.		MRP II: Manufacturing Resource Planning—5-Day
			MRP II: Manufacturing Resource Planning—5-Day
			MRP II: Manufacturing Resource Planning For Top Management
	Sales/Mktg. Mgr.		MRP II: Manufacturing Resource Planning For Top Management
	DP Mgr.		MRP II: Manufacturing Resource Planning—5-Day

MRP DETAILED IMPLEMENTATION PLAN

TASK	RESPONSIBLE	DATE	COMMENTS
B. Purchase or lease the MRP video courses for in-house education.	Team Leader	+1	These video courses will serve as the framework for all the educational courses in the following educational plan. The current library consists of 53 video tapes, approximately 33 hours of video taped education on MRP.
			The MRP video library is available through: The Oliver Wight Companies 5 Oliver Wight Drive Essex Junction, Vermont 05452 (802) 878-8161 or (800) 343-0625
C. Teachers course. Video education.	Team Leader	+1½	The team leader and all teachers go through the video courses to translate the general principles of MRP into the specifics of operation at the company. *Attendees:* All teachers. *Length:* Approx. 80 hrs.
D. Top Management Course. Video education.	Team Leader	+2+8	*Attendees:* Pres., all VPs, Plant Superintendent, others as appropriate. *Length:* Approx. 40 hrs.
E. Production and inventory control. Video education.	P&IC Mgr.	+2+8	*Attendees:* All people in P&IC. *Length:* Approx. 80 hrs.
Outside workshop	Master Scheduler	+3	Outside master scheduling workshop for one or more master schedulers. The workshop should be the equivalent of the one offered by The Oliver Wight Companies.

MRP DETAILED IMPLEMENTATION PLAN

TASK	RESPONSIBLE	DATE	COMMENTS
In-house training.	P&IC Mgr.	+7+8	*Attendees:* All people in P&IC. *Coverage:* All forms, reports, and documents that will be used by the people in P&IC. This includes a dry run of the system, sometimes called a "conference room pilot," to gain experience in using the reports and transactions.
F. Purchasing. Video education.	Purch. Mgr.	+2+8	*Attendees:* All people in purchasing. *Length:* Approx. 45 hrs.
Outside workshop.	Purch. Mgr. Buyers	+5	Outside purchasing workshop for one or more buyers. The workshop should be the equivalent of the one offered by The Oliver Wight Companies.
In-house training.	Purch. Mgr.	+7+8	*Attendees:* All people in purchasing. *Coverage:* All forms, reports, and documents that will be used by the people in purchasing. This includes a dry run of the system, sometimes called a "conference room pilot," to gain experience in using the reports and transactions.
G. Shop foreman. Video education.	VP Mfg. Plant Supt.	+2+8	*Attendees:* All shop foremen. *Length:* Approx. 40-45 hrs.
Outside workshop.	Shop Foreman	+5	Outside shop floor control and capacity requirements planning workshop. The workshop would be the equivalent of the one offered by The Oliver Wight Companies.
In-house training.	Plant Supt.	+7+8	*Attendees:* All shop foremen. *Coverage:* All forms, reports, and documents that will be used by the shop people. This includes a dry run using the documents.

MRP DETAILED IMPLEMENTATION PLAN

TASK	RESPONSIBLE	DATE	COMMENTS
H. Stockroom people. Video education.	Stockroom Mgr.	+2+4	*Attendees*: Anyone who will be making inventory transactions. *Length*: Approx. 15 hrs.
Outside workshop.	Stockroom Mgr.	+3	Outside inventory accuracy workshop for one or more stockroom managers. The workshop should be the equivalent of the one offered by The Oliver Wight Companies.
In-house training.	Stockroom Mgr.	+3	*Attendees*: Anyone who will be making inventory transactions. *Coverage*: All forms, reports, and documents that will be used in the inventory transaction system.
I. Sales and marketing. Video education.	Sales/Mktg. Mgr.	+3+8	*Attendees*: All sales and marketing people. This course is usually divided into two courses. One for those people in-house and one for those in district sales offices. *Length*: Approx. 25–30 hrs.
In-house training.	Sales/Mktg. Leader	+8	*Attendees*: All in-house sales and marketing people. *Coverage*: All forms, reports, and documents used in master scheduling and forecasting applicable to the sales and marketing people.

MRP DETAILED IMPLEMENTATION PLAN

TASK	RESPONSIBLE	DATE	COMMENTS
J. Engineering. Video education.	Engr. Mgr.	+2+8	*Attendees:* Anyone who will be working with bills of material or routings. *Length:* Approx. 30–40 hrs.
Outside workshop.	Engr. Mgr.	+3	Outside bill of material structuring workshop for the engineering manager and several of the engineers who will be structuring bills of material. The bill of material workshop should be the equivalent of the workshop offered by the Oliver Wight Companies.
In-house training.	Engr. Mgr.	+5	*Attendees:* Anyone who will be working with bills of material or routings. *Coverage:* All forms, reports, and documents that will be used to maintain bills of material and routings.
K. Data processing. Video education.	DP Mgr.	+2+8	*Attendees:* Anyone who will be working with the MRP programs or files. *Length:* Approx. 55 hrs.
L. Finance. Video education.	Mgr. Finance/ Accounting	+2+8	*Attendees:* All people in finance. *Length:* Approx. 35 hrs.
Outside workshop.	Mgr. Finance/ Accounting	+2+8	Outside finance and accounting workshop for one or more managers of finance and/or accounting. The workshop should be the equivalent of the one offered by The Oliver Wight Companies.
M. Lead men and setup men.	Shop Foremen	+2+8	*Attendees:* All setup or lead men. *Length:* Approx. 20 hrs.

MRP DETAILED IMPLEMENTATION PLAN

TASK	RESPONSIBLE	DATE	COMMENTS
N. Distribution center managers. Video education.	Distribution Mgr.	+2+8	*Attendees:* All distribution center or branch warehouse managers. *Length:* Approx. 20 hrs.
Outside workshop.	Distribution Mgr. DC Mgrs. Master Scheduler P&IC Mgr.	+3	Outside distribution resource planning workshop for the manager of distribution, one or more distribution center or branch warehouse managers, one or more master schedulers, P&IC manager. The workshop should be the equivalent of the one offered by The Oliver Wight Companies.
O. Distribution center employees. Video education.	DC Mgrs.	+3+8	*Attendees:* All distribution center employees. *Length:* Approx. 15 hrs.
P. Introduction to all direct labor employees.	VP Mfg. Plant Supt.	+3+8	*Attendees:* All direct labor employees. *Length:* Approx. 2 hrs.
Q. Anyone else affected by the system and not covered in the courses above.	Team Leader	+8	*Attendees:* As required. *Length:* As required.
4. Inventory accuracy.	Stockroom Mgr.	+8	This phase of the plan is aimed at bringing the inventory accuracy to 95% of the items within the counting error. This must be accomplished before the pilot program can be started. This includes distribution centers or branch warehouses.
A. Measure 100 parts as a starting point.	Stockroom Mgr.	+1	This will help assess the work that needs to be done to bring the inventory records to 95%.
B. Map out limited access to the stockroom areas.	Stockroom Mgr.	+1	Lay out any stockroom changes that are necessary to insure limited access.

MRP DETAILED IMPLEMENTATION PLAN

TASK	RESPONSIBLE	DATE	COMMENTS
C. Provide the tools for limited access and transaction recording.	Top Management Stockroom Mgr. Team Leader DP Mgr.	+3	A fence, enough stockroom people, adequate space, counting scales, transaction forms, labels, skids, etc.
D. Assign responsibility for the inventory accuracy.	Top Management	+3	The inventory manager and his people are now responsible for the inventory accuracy. Change job descriptions where necessary.
E. Start counting a control group of 100 parts.	Stockroom Mgr.	+3	Control group parts are counted once every ten days. Any inventory errors are investigated to find the cause of the error.
F. Each ten days a report is published showing the results of the control group.	Stockroom Mgr.	+3 on	The report should show the history of the inventory accuracy and the cause of the errors.
G. Start cycle counting all inventory items.	Stockroom Mgr.	+5 on	All parts are counted periodically. A simple method would be to count A and B items twice a year, and the C items once a year.
H. Bring the inventory accuracy to 95% of the parts within counting error.	Stockroom Mgr.	+8	As measured by the results of cycle counting the items in inventory, and not based only on the control group items.
5. Bill of material accuracy.	Engr. Mgr. P&IC Mgr.	+8	This phase of the plan is aimed at bringing bill of material accuracy to 98%. The tasks in this phase must be completed before the pilot program can begin. Both design and production engineering should participate in structuring the bills of material.

MRP DETAILED IMPLEMENTATION PLAN

TASK	RESPONSIBLE	DATE	COMMENTS
A. Measure 100 bills of material as a starting point.	Engineering	+3	This will help assess the work that needs to be done to eliminate errors from the bills of material.
B. Decide and assign responsibility for the accuracy of bills of material.	Top Management	+3	This may involve centralizing some responsibilities and setting up procedures to control the flow of documents if these are not already present.
C. Verify the bills of material for correct part numbers and quantities per assembly.	Engineering	+8	This requires either a line-by-line audit or an exception system, like stockroom pulls, to point out bill of material errors. Either method must highlight and correct any errors in component part numbers or quantities per assembly.
D. Verify the bills of material to show the correct structure of the product.	Engineering	+8	This requires restructuring the bills where necessary to show: 1. The way material moves on the shop floor. 2. Raw materials on the bills of material. 3. Modules or self-consumed assemblies where needed.
E. Decide on and implement bill of material policies.	Top Management Engineering P&IC	+5	Policies: 1. Engineering change procedure. 2. Documenting new or special products.
6. Item analysis.	P&IC Mgr.	+8	This phase of the plan covers the verification or assignment of the ordering rules.
A. Measure 100 items as a starting point.	P&IC Purchasing Team Leader	+1	The parts are checked for correct lead times, ordering quantities, and safety stock (if applicable). This measurement will help assess the work that needs to be done.

MRP DETAILED IMPLEMENTATION PLAN

TASK	RESPONSIBLE	DATE	COMMENTS
B. Agree upon and assign responsibility for the ordering rules.	P&IC Purchasing	+2	Responsibilities depend on how purchasing fits into the organization and whether or not the planner/buyer concept is used.
C. Verify or establish ordering policies.	P&IC Purchasing	+8	Decide between fixed order policy or lot-for-lot ordering. Dynamic order policies like part period balancing are not recommended.
D. Verify or establish order quantities and order modifiers.	P&IC Purchasing	+8	Assign order quantities for fixed order policy items. Modifiers should be assigned where they are appropriate.
E. Verify or establish lead times.	P&IC Purchasing	+8	*Manufactured parts:* 1. Use simple scheduling rules. 2. Be consistent. *Purchased parts:* 1. Use current lead times.
F. Verify or establish safety stock levels.	P&IC Purchasing	+8	*Independent demand items:* 1. Consistent with the master schedule policy. *Dependent demand items:* 1. In special circumstances.
7. Master production schedule preparation.	Top Management Marketing P&IC Shop Management	+8	This phase of the plan covers the work required to set up a working master production schedule. Must include resource requirements planning.
A. Develop a production planning function.	Top Management Marketing P&IC Shop Management	+6	Production planning is basic strategic planning to develop a statement of production which is in families of products and by months.

MRP DETAILED IMPLEMENTATION PLAN

TASK	RESPONSIBLE	DATE	COMMENTS
B. Develop a master scheduling function.	P&IC	+6	Master scheduling takes the production plan and translates it into a specific statement of production. The master schedule is a statement of production in specific item numbers and by weeks.
C. Develop a master schedule policy.	Top Management Marketing P&IC Shop Management	+6	The master schedule policy should cover the following points for both production planning and master scheduling: 1. Procedure for changing the production plan or master production schedule. This procedure should include who can request a change, how the proposed change is investigated, and who should approve it before it is implemented. 2. Periodic reviews of the forecast and actual sales, also the master schedule and the actual production. The purpose of these reviews is to determine whether or not the production plan or master production schedule should be changed.
D. Begin operating the production plan and master production schedule.	Top Management Marketing P&IC Shop Management	+8	The first production plan and master production schedule are developed.

MRP DETAILED IMPLEMENTATION PLAN

TASK	RESPONSIBLE	DATE	COMMENTS
8. Systems work and software selection.	DP Mgr.	+8	This phase of the plan outlines the work that needs to be done in selecting software and accomplishing the systems work and programming for the MRP system.
A. Review and select software to be used.	Data Processing P&IC Shop Management	+2	Software should be evaluated using the software evaluations from: The Oliver Wight Companies 5 Oliver Wight Drive Essex Junction, Vermont 05452 (802) 878-8161 or (800) 343-0625
B. Systems work, programming, and testing of inventory transactions.	Data Processing	+5	Issues, receipts, cycle counting.
C. Systems work, programming, and testing of bills of material.	Data Processing	+6	Normal bill of material functions.
D. Systems work, programming, and testing of scheduled receipts.	Data Processing	+6½	Scheduling receipts: 1. Manufacturing orders. 2. Purchase orders. 3. Distribution orders.
E. Systems work, programming, and testing of the MRP logic.	Data Processing	+8	Any modifications that need to be made.
F. Systems work, programming, and testing of the master schedule system.	Data Processing	+8	Master scheduling and production planning support.
G. Agree on time schedules and cutoff times.	Data Processing	+6	Times for reports, transactions and cutoff times for transactions to the system.

MRP DETAILED IMPLEMENTATION PLAN

TASK	RESPONSIBLE	DATE	COMMENTS
9. Pre-installation tasks.	P&IC Mgr. Team Leader	+8	This phase of the plan covers the tasks that immediately precede the pilot program. Must include some form of shop dispatching.
A. Set up planner structure and part responsibilities.	P&IC	+8	Which planners are responsible for which groups of parts? Decide among vertical or horizontal responsibility: 1. Vertical product line-oriented. 2. Horizontal department-oriented.
B. Set up procedures for handling both top down and bottom up closed loop planning.	P&IC Shop Foremen Purchasing	+8	Specific procedures for rescheduling, order release, and feedback of anticipated delays.
C. Physical cleanup.	P&IC Shop Foremen Purchasing	+8	Physical cleanup of the shop floor to insure that each open order has the required component parts, and that all parts on the floor are on an open order. Parts not covered by a shop order should be returned to the stockroom. All manufacturing orders and purchase orders should be verified.
10. Pilot program.	Everyone involved so far	+8+9	This is the pilot program. It is a trial run of the system on one or a group of product lines that total several hundred part numbers. The purpose is to verify that the system is giving correct information.
A. Monitor the critical measurements.	Team Leader	+8+9	Verify that the system is providing correct information and that people are comfortable using the system.

MRP DETAILED IMPLEMENTATION PLAN

TASK	RESPONSIBLE	DATE	COMMENTS
11. Cutover.	Everyone involved so far.	+9+12	This phase of the plan outlines the sequence that is used to move from the pilot program to full implementation on all product lines.
A. Group the remaining product lines into three or four divisions.	P&IC	+9	Divisions should contain product lines that are similar or share common parts.
B. Bring each division onto MRP, one division at a time.	P&IC	+9+12	As each division is put onto MRP, set up planner coverage so the product lines involved get intense planner coverage until they are quieted down.

END OF FIRST MAJOR SECTION IN IMPLEMENTATION

TASK	RESPONSIBLE	DATE	COMMENTS
12. Training for shop floor control, capacity requirements planning, input/output control, and purchasing.	Shop Management	+15	This phase of the plan outlines the training for shop floor control, capacity requirements planning and purchasing. This training has the same objectives and the same basic course outline as the MRP training covered previously.
A. Shop Foremen. In-house training.	Plant Supt.	+15	*Attendees:* All shop foremen. *Coverage:* All forms, reports, and documents that will be used in the shop floor control and capacity requirements planning systems.
B. Planners. In-house training.	P&IC Mgr.	+15	*Attendees:* All planners that will be working with the shop people. *Coverage:* All forms, reports, and documents that will be used in the shop floor control and capacity requirements planning systems.

MRP DETAILED IMPLEMENTATION PLAN

TASK	RESPONSIBLE	DATE	COMMENTS
C. Shop dispatchers. In-house training.	Shop Foremen	+15	*Attendees:* All shop dispatchers. *Coverage:* All forms, reports and documents that will be used in the shop floor control and capacity requirements planning systems.
D. Purchasing. In-house training.	Purch. Mgr.	+15	*Attendees:* All purchasing people. *Coverage:* All forms, reports and documents that will be used in vendor follow-up and vendor negotiation.
13. Routing accuracy.	Shop Foremen Prod. Engr.	+15	This phase of the plan outlines the work that needs to be done to get routing accuracy to 95%.
A. Measure 100 routings as a starting point.	Shop Foremen Prod. Engr.	+10	This will help assess the work that needs to be done to eliminate errors from the routings.
B. Decide on and assign responsibility for the accuracy of the routings.	Top Management	+11	This may involve centralizing some responsibilities or defining areas of responsibilities if these do not already exist.
C. Verify that the routings show the operations correctly.	Shop Foremen Prod. Engr.	+15	This requires either a line-by-line audit of the routing or an exception system to point out routing errors. Either method must highlight and correct the errors in the routings. The routings should be verified for the following: 1. The correct operations and work centers. 2. The correct operation sequence. 3. A reasonable standard that can be used in scheduling.

MRP DETAILED IMPLEMENTATION PLAN

TASK	RESPONSIBLE	DATE	COMMENTS
14. Work center identification.	Shop Foremen Prod. Engr.	+15	This phase of the plan outlines the simple steps that are required to define and classify the work centers.
A. Identify work centers.	Shop Foremen Prod. Engr.	+15	Decide which machines or groups of machines will be called work centers. In some cases a single machine will be a work center. In others, a group of similar machines will be a work center.
15. Systems work.	DP Mgr.	+15	This phase of the plan outlines the systems work and programming that must be done for shop floor control and capacity requirements planning.
A. Systems work, programming, and testing of shop floor control.	Data Processing	+15	Shop floor control functions.
B. Systems work, programming, and testing of capacity requirements planning.	Data Processing	+15	Capacity requirements planning functions.
C. Systems work, programming, and testing of input/output control.	Data Processing	+15	Input/output control report.
D. Systems work, programming, and testing for purchasing.	Data Processing	+15	Vendor follow-up and vendor negotiation reports.

MRP DETAILED IMPLEMENTATION PLAN

TASK	RESPONSIBLE	DATE	COMMENTS
16. Implementation of shop floor control.	Shop Foremen P&IC	+15 +16	The implementation of shop floor control uses a pilot program since new transactions and disciplines are being used on the shop floor.
A. Implement shop floor control on a pilot group of parts.	Shop Foremen P&IC	+15	The pilot should be large enough to provide one hundred or so shop orders. It is also helpful to use a product line that will create shop orders under shop floor control in all departments.
B. Implement shop floor control on the remaining items.	Shop Foremen P&IC	+15½	Cut over remaining items.
17. Implement capacity requirements planning, input/output control, and purchasing.	Shop Foremen P&IC Purch. Mgr.	+16	This is a simple implementation. Capacity requirements planning, input/output control, and purchasing negotiation reports are simply stated.

END OF SECOND MAJOR SECTION IN IMPLEMENTATION

MRP DETAILED IMPLEMENTATION PLAN

TASK	RESPONSIBLE	DATE	COMMENTS
18. Training for financial planning and simulation.	Mgr. Finance/ Accounting, P&IC Mgr.	+18	This phase of the plan outlines the training for financial planning and simulations. This training has the same objectives and the same basic course outline as the MRP training covered previously.
A. Finance and accounting. In-house training.	Mgr. Finance/ Accounting	+18	*Attendees:* People in finance and accounting. *Coverage:* All forms, reports, and documents that will be used.
B. Production and inventory control. In-house training.	P&IC Mgr.	+18	*Attendees:* People in P&IC. *Coverage:* Differences between simulations and normal operation of the system.
19. Develop financial planning numbers.	Mgr. Finance/ Accounting	+18	These numbers are used to do inventory projections, cash flow projections, and fixed overhead allocations. Numbers include: 1. Cost by item. 2. Labor costs. 3. Machinery operating costs. 4. Fixed overhead allocations by work center, group of work centers, or departments.

MRP DETAILED IMPLEMENTATION PLAN

TASK	RESPONSIBLE	DATE	COMMENTS

20. Implement financial planning and simulations.	Mgr. Finance/ Accounting P&IC Mgr.	+18	No pilot is needed. Begin running the programs and verify the numbers before using for decisions. Types of simulations available include:
			1. Changed master production schedule:
			  A. Material impact.
			  B. Capacity impact.
			  C. Financial impact.
			  D. Marketing impact.
			2. Make/Buy simulations.
			3. Different forecast—same MPS.
			4. Sales promotions—same or different MPS.
			5. New product introductions.

Darryl Landvater
The Oliver Wight Companies
5 Oliver Wight Drive
Essex Junction, Vermont 05452
(802) 878-8161 or (800) 343-0625

The Oliver Wight Companies' Services

Preparing yourself to implement a Class A MRP II system requires careful study of a huge amount of information, far more than could be included in this or any other book. The Oliver Wight Companies can provide further assistance in getting ready, including books on the subject, live education, videotaped in-plant education, consultation, and reviews of commercially available software packages.

OLIVER WIGHT LIMITED PUBLICATIONS, INC.

Oliver Wight Limited Publications, Inc. was created in 1981 to publish books on MRP II, written by leading educators and consultants in the field. Titles include:

Manufacturing Resource Planning: MRP II—Unlocking America's Productivity Potential by the late Oliver W. Wight. Co-published in 1984 with Van Nostrand Reinhold.

The Executive's Guide to Successful MRP II by the late Oliver W. Wight. Co-published in 1981 with Prentice-Hall.

DRP: Distribution Resource Planning—Distribution Management's Most Powerful Tool by Andre J. Martin. Co-published with Prentice-Hall, Inc. in 1983.

Focus Forecasting: Computer Techniques for Inventory Control by Bernard T. Smith. Published in 1984.

For more information, or to order publications, contact:

Oliver Wight Limited Publications, Inc.
5 Oliver Wight Drive
Essex Junction, VT 05452
800-343-0625 or 802-878-8161

OLIVER WIGHT EDUCATION ASSOCIATES

OWEA is made up of a group of independent MRP II educators
and consultants around the world who share a common philosophy and common goals. Classes directed towards both upper-
and middle-level management are being taught in various locations around the U.S. and Canada, as well as abroad. For a
Detailed Class Brochure, listing course descriptions, instructors,
costs, dates, and locations, or for the name of a recommended
consultant in your area, please contact:

Oliver Wight Education Associates
P.O. Box 435
Newbury, NH 03255
800-258-3862 or 603-763-5926

OLIVER WIGHT VIDEO PRODUCTIONS, INC.

The Oliver Wight Video Library offers companies the video-based
materials they need to teach the "critical mass" of their employees
about the principles of MRP II. The Library is accompanied by
Course Guides to assist instructors in directing the discussion
sessions that supplement the information on tape. For more information on obtaining the Oliver Wight Video Library, contact.

Oliver Wight Video Productions, Inc.
5 Oliver Wight Drive
Essex Junction, VT 05452
800-343-0625 or 802-878-8161

OLIVER WIGHT SOFTWARE RESEARCH, INC.

To help you make the right choice about software in a reasonable
length of time, Oliver Wight Software Research (formerly known

as Manufacturing Software Systems, Inc.) offers Software Evaluations and Audits, comprehensive reviews of the capabilities of many of the most popular packages on the market today. All reviews are based on the MRP II Standard Software System Description, a research document outlining all the functions required to perform Manufacturing Resource Planning. The Standard System is also available for use as an in-house evaluation and teaching aid. OWSR also offers a three-day course entitled, "Systems, Data, and Software Selection," as well as Evaluation Consulting Support, to guide companies through the in-house evaluation process.

For more information, contact:

Oliver Wight Software Research, Inc.
5 Oliver Wight Drive
Essex Junction, VT 05452
800-343-0625 or 802-878-8161

Bibliography

Berry, William, Thomas E. Vollmann, and D. Clay Whybark. *Master Production Scheduling: Principles and Practices.* Falls Church, VA: American Production and Inventory Control Society, 1979.

Martin, Andre. *DRP: Distribution Resource Planning—Distribution Management's Most Powerful Tool.* Essex Junction, VT: Oliver Wight Limited Publications, Inc., 1983.

Morgan, James. "MRP II—that powerful tool!" *Purchasing,* 6 September 1984, pp. 109–115, 4 October 1984, pp. 59–64, 18 October 1984, pp. 129–132.

Smith, Bernard T. *Focus Forecasting: Computer Techniques for Inventory Control.* Boston: CBI Publishing Company, Inc., 1978.

Wight, Oliver W. *The Executive's Guide to Successful MRP II.* Essex Junction, VT: Oliver Wight Limited Publications, Inc., 1981.

———. *Manufacturing Resource Planning: MRP II—Unlocking America's Productivity Potential.* Revised Edition. Essex Junction, VT: Oliver Wight Limited Publications, Inc., 1981.

———. *Production and Inventory Management in the Computer Age.* Boston: CBI Publishing Company, Inc., 1974.

Glossary

Many of the terms found in this glossary have been drawn or adapted from the *APICS Dictionary,* Thomas F. Wallace, Editor. Reprinted with permission, American Production & Inventory Control Society, Inc., *APICS Dictionary, Fifth Edition,* 1984.

ABC CLASSIFICATION   Classification of the items in an inventory in decreasing order of annual dollar volume or other criteria. This array is then split into three classes, called A, B, and C. Class A contains the items with the highest annual dollar volume and receives the most attention. The medium Class B receives less attention, and Class C, which contains the low-dollar volume items, is controlled routinely. The ABC principle is that effort saved through relaxed controls on low-value items will be applied to reduce inventories of high-value items.

ACTION MESSAGE   An output of an MRP II system that identifies the need for and the type of action to be taken to correct a current or a potential problem. Examples of action messages are "Release Order," "Reschedule Out," "Cancel," etc.

ALLOCATION   In an MRP II system, an allocated item is one for which a picking order has been released to the stockroom but not yet sent out of the stockroom. It is an "uncashed" stockroom requisition.

ANTICIPATED DELAY REPORT   A report, normally issued by both manfacturing and purchasing to the material planning function, regarding jobs or purchase orders which will not be completed on time, why not, and when they will be completed. This is an essential ingredient of a closed loop system. Except perhaps in very large companies, the anticipated delay report is manually prepared.

AUTOMATIC RESCHEDULING   Allowing the computer to automatically change due dates on scheduled receipts when it detects that due dates and required dates are out of phase. Automatic rescheduling is not recommended.

AVAILABLE TO PROMISE   The uncommitted portion of a company's inventory or planned production. This figure is frequently calculated from the master production schedule and is maintained as a tool for order promising.

BACKFLUSH   The deduction from inventory of the component parts used in an assembly or subassembly by exploding the bill of materials by the production count of assemblies produced. *See* Post-deduct inventory transaction processing.

BACKLOG   All of the customer orders booked, i.e., received but not yet shipped. Sometimes referred to as "open orders" or the "order board."

BACK SCHEDULING   A technique for calculating operation start and due dates. The schedule is computed starting with the due date for the order and working backward to determine the required completion dates for each operation.

BILL OF MATERIAL   A listing of all the subassemblies, intermediates, parts and raw materials, etc. that go into a parent item, showing the quantity of each component required. May also be called "formula," "recipe," or "ingredients list" in certain industries.

BUCKETED SYSTEM   An MRP, DRP or other time-phased system in which all time-phased data are accumulated into time periods or "buckets." If the period of accumulation would be one week, then the system would be said to have weekly buckets.

BUCKETLESS SYSTEM   An MRP II, DRP or other time-phased system in which all time-phased data are processed, stored and displayed using dated records rather than defined time periods or "buckets."

BUSINESS PLAN   A statement of income projections, costs and profits usually accompanied by budgets and a projected balance sheet as well as a cash flow (source and application of funds) statement. It is usually stated in terms of dollars only. The business plan and the production plan, although frequently stated in different terms, should be in agreement with each other.

CAD/CAM   The integration of Computer Aided Design and Computer Aided Manufacturing to achieve automation from design through manufacturing.

CAPACITY REQUIREMENTS PLANNING (CRP)   The process of determining how much labor and/or machine resources are required to accomplish the tasks of production, and making plans to provide these resources. Open shop orders, as well as planned orders in the MRP system, are input to CRP which "translates" these orders into hours of work by work center by time period. In earlier years, the computer portion of CRP was called "infinite loading," a misnomer.

CLOSED LOOP MRP   A system built around material requirements planning and also including the additional planning functions of production planning, master production scheduling, and capacity requirements planning. Further, once the planning phase is complete and the plans have been accepted as realistic and attainable, the execution functions come into play. These include the shop floor control functions of input/output measurement, dispatching, plus anticipated delay reports from both the shop and vendors, vendor scheduling, etc. The term "closed loop" implies that not only is each of these elements included in the overall system but also that there is feedback from the execution functions so that the planning can be kept valid at all times.

COMMON PARTS BILL (OF MATERIAL)   A type of planning bill which groups all common components for a product or family of products into one bill of material.

CUMULATIVE LEAD TIME   The longest length of time involved to accomplish the activity in question. For any item planned through MRP it is found by reviewing each bill of material path below the item, and whichever path adds up to the greatest number defines cumulative material lead time. Also called aggregate lead time, stacked lead time, composite lead time, critical path lead time.

CYCLE COUNTING   A physical inventory-taking technique where inventory is counted on a periodic schedule rather than once a year. For example, a cycle inventory count may be taken when an item reaches its reorder point, when new stock is received, or on a regular basis usually more frequently for high-value fast-moving items and less frequently for low-value or slow-moving items. Most effective cycle counting systems require the counting of a certain number of items every work day.

DAMPENERS A technique within material requirements planning used to suppress the reporting of certain action messages created during the computer processing of MRP. Extensive use of dampeners is not recommended.

DEMAND A need for a particular product or component. The demand could come from any number of sources, i.e., customer order, forecast, interplant, branch warehouse, service part, or to manufacture the next higher level. *See* Dependent demand, Independent demand.

DEMAND MANAGEMENT The function of recognizing and managing all of the demands for products to ensure that the master scheduler is aware of them. It encompasses the activities of forecasting, order entry, order promising, branch warehouse requirements, interplant requirements, interplant orders, and service parts requirements.

DEMONSTRATED CAPACITY Capacity calculated from actual performance data, usually number of items produced times standard hours per item plus the standard set-up time for each job.

DEPENDENT DEMAND Demand is considered dependent when it comes from production schedules for other items. These demands should be calculated, not forecasted. A given item may have both dependent and independent demand at any given time. *See* Independent demand.

DIRECT-DEDUCT INVENTORY TRANSACTION PROCESSING A method of doing bookkeeping which decreases the book (computer) inventory of an item as material is issued from stock, and increases the book inventory as material is received into stock. The key concept here is that the book record is updated coincident with the movement of material out of or into stock. As a result, the book record is a representation of what is physically in stock.

DISPATCH LIST   A listing of manufacturing orders in priority sequence according to the dispatching rules. The dispatch list is usually communicated to the manufacturing floor via hard copy or CRT display, and contains detailed information on priority, location, quantity, and the capacity requirements of the manufacturing order by operation. Dispatch lists are normally generated daily and oriented by work center. Also called the "daily foremen's report."

DISTRIBUTION CENTER   A warehouse with finished goods and/or service items. A typical company, for example, might have a manufacturing facility in Philadelphia and distribution centers in Atlanta, Dallas, Los Angeles, San Francisco, and Chicago. The term "distribution center" is synonymous with the term "branch warehouse," although the former has become more commonly used recently. When there is a warehouse that serves a group of satellite warehouses, this is usually called a regional distribution center.

DISTRIBUTION REQUIREMENTS PLANNING   The function of determining the needs to replenish inventory at branch warehouses. A time-phased order-point approach is used, where the planned orders at the branch warehouse level are "exploded" via MRP logic to become gross requirements on the supplying source. In the case of multilevel distribution networks, this explosion process can continue down through the various levels of master warehouse, factory warehouse, etc., and become input to the master production schedule. Demand on the supplying source(s) is recognized as dependent, and standard MRP logic applies.

DISTRIBUTION RESOURCE PLANNING (DRP)   The extension of Distribution Requirements Planning into the planning of the key resources contained in a distribution system: warehouse space, manpower, money, trucks and freight cars, etc.

FINAL ASSEMBLY SCHEDULE (FAS)   Also referred to as the "finishing schedule" as it may include other operations than simply the final operation. It is a schedule of end items either to replenish finished goods inventory or to finish the product for a make-to-order product. For make-to-order products, it is prepared after receipt of a customer order, is constrained by the availability of material and capacity, and it schedules the operations required to complete the product from the level where it is stocked (or master scheduled) to the end item level.

FINITE LOADING   Conceptually, the term means putting no more work into a work center than it can be expected to execute. The specific term usually refers to a computer technique that involves automatic shop priority revision in order to level load operation-by-operation. Successful applications of finite loading are very difficult to find.

FIRM PLANNED ORDER   A planned order that can be frozen in quantity and time. The computer is not allowed to change it; this is the responsibility of the planner in charge of the item. This technique can aid planners to respond to material and capacity problems by firming up selected planned orders. Firm planned orders are also the normal method of stating the master production schedule.

FIXED ORDER QUANTITY   An order quantity technique where the same quantity is planned to be ordered each time.

FLOW SHOP   A shop in which machines and operators handle a standard, usually uninterrupted material flow. The operators tend to perform the same operations for each production run. A flow shop is often referred to as a mass production shop, or is said to have a continuous manufacturing layout. The shop layout (arrangement of machines, benches, assembly lines, etc.) is designed to facilitate a product "flow." The process industries (chemicals, oil, paint, etc.) are extreme examples of flow shops. Each product, though variable in material specifications, uses the same flow pattern through the shop. See: job shop.

FOCUS FORECASTING   A system that allows the user to simulate the effectiveness of numerous forecasting techniques, thereby being able to select the most effective one.

FULL PEGGING   Refers to the ability of a system to automatically trace requirements for a given component all the way up to its ultimate end item (or contract number).

GENERALLY ACCEPTED MANUFACTURING PRACTICES   A group of practices and principles, independent of any one set of techniques, which defines how a manufacturing company should be managed. Included are such elements as the need for data accuracy, frequent communications between marketing and manufacturing, top management control of the production planning process, systems capable of validly translating high-level plans into detailed schedules, etc.

GROUP TECHNOLOGY   An engineering and manufacturing philosophy which identifies the "sameness" of parts, equipment or processes. It provides for rapid retrieval of existing designs and anticipates a cellular-type production equipment layout.

HEDGE   1) In master production scheduling, a quantity of stock used to protect against uncertainty in demand. The hedge is similar to safety stock, except that a hedge has the dimension of timing as well as amount. 2) In purchasing, any purchase or sale transaction having as its purpose the elimination of the negative aspects of price fluctuations.

INDEPENDENT DEMAND   Demand for an item is considered independent when such demand is unrelated to the demand for other items. Demand for finished goods and service parts are examples of independent demand.

INFINITE LOADING   *See* Capacity requirements planning.

INPUT/OUTPUT CONTROL   A technique for capacity control where actual output from a work center is compared with the planned output (as developed by CRP and approved by Manufacturing). The input is also monitored to see if it corresponds with plans so that work centers will not be expected to generate output when jobs are not available to work on.

INTERPLANT DEMAND   Material to be shipped to another plant or division within the corporation. Although it is not a customer order, it is usually handled by the master production scheduling system in a similar manner.

ITEM RECORD   The "master" record for an item. Typically it contains identifying and descriptive data, control values (lead times, lot order quantities, etc.) and may contain data on inventory status, requirements, and planned orders. Item records are linked together by bill of material records (or product structure records), thus defining the bill of material.

JOB SHOP   A functional organization whose departments or work centers are organized around particular types of equipment or operations, such as drilling, forging, spinning, or assembly. Products move through departments by individual shop orders.

JUST-IN-TIME   In the narrow sense, a method of execution designed to result in minimum inventory by having material arrive at each operation just in time to be used. In the broad sense, it refers to all the activities of manufacturing which make the just-in-time movement of material possible, with the ultimate goal being elimination of waste. Just-in-time is possible via MRP II or, in some cases, via Kanban.

KANBAN   A scheduling approach which uses standard containers with a card attached to each. Developed in Japan, it has been used in certain highly repetitive manufacturing environments to achieve Just-In-Time. Loosely translated, Kanban means "card," or more literally, "billboard" or "sign."

LEAD TIME   A span of time required to perform an activity. In a logistics context, the activity in question is normally the procurement of materials and/or products either from an outside supplier or from one's own manufacturing facility. The individual components of any given lead time can include some or all of the following: order preparation time, queue time, move or transportation time, receiving and inspection time.

LEVEL   Every part of assembly in a product structure is assigned a level code signifying the relative level in which that part or assembly is used within that product structure. Normally, the end items are assigned level "0" and the components/subassemblies going into it are level "1" and so on. The MRP explosion process starts from level "0" and proceeds downwards one level at a time.

LOAD   The amount of scheduled work ahead of a manufacturing facility, usually expressed in terms of hours of work or units of production.

LOGISTICS   In an industrial context, this term refers to the functions of obtaining and distributing material and product. In a military sense (where it has greater usage), its meaning can also include the transportation of personnel.

LOT-FOR-LOT   An order quantity technique in MRP which generates planned orders in quantities equal to the net requirements in each period. Also called discrete, one-for-one.

MACHINE LOADING   The accumulation by work centers of the hours generated from the scheduling of operations for released orders by time period. Machine loading differs from capacity requirements planning in that it does not use the planned orders from MRP but operates solely for scheduled receipts. As such, it has very limited usefulness.

MAKE-TO-ORDER PRODUCT   The end item is finished after receipt of a customer order. Frequently, long lead-time components are planned prior to the order arriving in order to reduce the delivery time to the customer. Where options or other subassemblies are stocked prior to customer orders arriving, the term "assemble-to-order" is frequently used.

MAKE-TO-STOCK PRODUCT   The end item is shipped from finished goods "off the shelf," and therefore, is finished prior to a customer order arriving.

MANUFACTURING RESOURCE PLANNING (MRP II)   A method for the effective planning of all resources of a manufacturing company. Ideally, it addresses operational planning in units, financial planning in dollars, and has a simulation capability to answer "what if" questions. It is made up of a variety of functions, each linked together: business planning, production planning, master production scheduling, material requirements planning, capacity requirements planning and the execution support systems for capacity and material. Output from these systems would be integrated with financial reports such as the business plan, purchase commitment reports, shipping budget, inventory projections in dollars, etc. Manufacturing Resource Planning is a direct outgrowth and extension of closed loop MRP. MRP II has also been defined, validly, as a management system based on network scheduling. Also, and perhaps best, as organized common sense.

MASTER PRODUCTION SCHEDULE (MPS) The anticipated build schedule. The master scheduler maintains this schedule and, in turn, it becomes a set of planning numbers which "drives" MRP. It represents what the company plans to produce expressed in specific configurations, quantities and dates. The master production schedule must take into account customer orders and forecasts, backlog, availability of material, availability of capacity, management policy and goals, etc.

MATERIAL REQUIREMENTS PLANNING (MRP) A set of techniques which uses bills of material, inventory data and the master production schedule to calculate requirements for materials. It makes recommendations to release replenishment orders for material. Further, since it is time phased, it makes recommendations to reschedule open orders when due dates and need dates are not in phase. Originally seen as merely a better way to order inventory, today it is thought of primarily as a scheduling technique, i.e., a method for establishing and maintaining valid due dates on orders. It is the foundation for closed loop MRP.

MATERIALS MANAGEMENT An organizational structure which groups the functions related to the complete cycle of material flow, from the purchase and internal control of production materials to the planning and control of work-in-process to the warehousing, shipping and distribution of the finished product.

MODULAR BILL (OF MATERIAL) A type of planning bill which is arranged in product modules or options. Often used in companies where the product has many optional features, e.g., automobiles. *See* Planning bill.

MURPHY'S LAW A tongue-in-cheek observation which states: "If anything can go wrong, it will."

NET CHANGE MRP A method of processing material requirements planning on the computer whereby the material plan is continually retained in the computer. Whenever there is a change in requirements, open order or inventory status, bills of material, etc., a partial explosion is made only for those parts affected by the change.

NET REQUIREMENTS   In MRP, the net requirements for a part or an assembly are derived as a result of netting gross requirements against inventory on hand and the scheduled receipts. Net requirements, lot sized and offset for lead time, become planned orders.

ON-HAND BALANCE   The quantity shown in the inventory records as being physically in stock.

OPEN ORDER   An active manufacturing order or purchase order. *See* Scheduled receipts.

OPTION   A choice or feature offered to customers for customizing the end product. In many companies, the term "option" means a mandatory choice, i.e., the customer must select from one of the available choices. For example, in ordering a new car, the customer must specify an engine (option) but need not necessarily select an air conditioner.

ORDER ENTRY   The process of accepting and translating what a customer wants into terms used by the manufacturer. This can be as simple as creating shipping documents for a finished goods product to a far more complicated series of activities including engineering effort for make-to-order products.

ORDER PROMISING   The process of making a delivery commitment, i.e., answering the question "When can you ship?" For make-to-order products, this usually involves a check of material and capacity availability.

ORDER QUANTITY   The amount of an item to be ordered. Also called lot size.

PEGGING   In MRP, pegging displays, for a given item, the details of the sources of its gross requirements and/or allocations. Pegging can be thought of as "live" where-used information.

PERIOD ORDER QUANTITY   An order quantity technique under which the order quantity will be equal to the net requirements for a given number of periods (e.g., weeks) into the future. Also called days' supply, weeks' supply, fixed period.

PICKING The process of issuing components to the production floor on a job-by-job basis. Also called kitting.

PICKING LIST A document which is used to pick manufacturing orders, listing the components and quantities required.

PLANNED ORDER A suggested order quantity and due date created by MRP processing, when it encounters net requirements. Planned orders are created by the computer, exist only within the computer, and may be changed or deleted by the computer during subsequent MRP processing if conditions change. Planned orders at one level will be exploded into gross requirements for components at the next lower level. Planned orders also serve as input to capacity requirements planning, along with scheduled receipts, to show the total capacity requirements in future time periods.

PLANNER/BUYER *See* Vendor scheduler.

PLANNING BILL (OF MATERIAL) An artificial grouping of items and/or events, in bill of material format, used to facilitate master scheduling and/or material planning. A modular bill of material is one type of planning bill.

POST-DEDUCT INVENTORY TRANSACTION PROCESSING A method of doing inventory bookkeeping where the book (computer) inventory of components is reduced only after completion of activity on their upper level parent or assembly. This approach has the disadvantage of a built-in differential between the book record and what is physically in stock. Also called backflush.

PRE-DEDUCT INVENTORY TRANSACTION PROCESSING A method of doing inventory bookkeeping where the book (computer) inventory of components is reduced prior to issue, at the time of scheduled receipt for their parent or assembly is created. This approach has the disadvantage of a built-in differential between the book record and what is physically in stock.

PRODUCT STRUCTURE *See* Bill of material.

PRODUCTION PLANNING The function of setting the overall level of manufacturing output. Its prime purpose is to establish production rates that will achieve management's objective in terms of raising or lowering inventories or backlogs, while usually attempting to keep the production force relatively stable. The production plan is usually stated in broad terms (e.g., product groupings, families of products). It must extend through a planning horizon sufficient to plan the labor, equipment, facilities, material and finances required to accomplish the production plan. Various units of measure are used by different companies to express the plan such as standard hours, tonnage, labor operators, units, pieces, etc. As this plan affects all company functions, it is normally prepared with information from marketing, manufacturing, engineering, finance, materials, etc. In turn, the production plan becomes management's authorization for the master scheduler to convert into a more detailed plan.

PROJECTED AVAILABLE BALANCE   The inventory balance projected out into the future. It is the running sum of on-hand inventory, minus requirements, plus scheduled receipts and (usually) planned orders.

QUEUE   A waiting line. In manufacturing the jobs at a given work center waiting to be processed. As queues increase, so do average lead times and work-in-process inventories.

QUEUE TIME   The amount of time a job waits at a work center before set-up or work is performed on the job. Queue time is one element of total manufacturing lead time. Increases in queue time result in direct increases to manufacturing lead time.

REGENERATION MRP   A method of processing material requirements planning on the computer whereby the master production schedule is totally re-exploded down through all bills of material, at least once per week to maintain valid priorities. New requirements and planned orders are completely "regenerated" at that time.

REPETITIVE MANUFACTURING   Production of discrete units, planned and executed via schedule, usually at relatively high speeds and volumes. Material tends to move in a sequential flow. *See* Flow shop.

RESCHEDULING ASSUMPTION   A fundamental piece of MRP logic which assumes that existing open orders can be rescheduled in nearer time periods far more easily than new orders can be released and received. As a result, planned order receipts are not created until all scheduled receipts have been applied to cover gross requirements.

RESOURCE REQUIREMENTS PLANNING   *See* Rough-cut capacity planning.

ROUGH-CUT CAPACITY PLANNING   The process of converting the production plan and/or the master production schedule into capacity needs for key resources: manpower, machinery, warehouse space, vendors' capabilities and in some cases, money. Product load profiles are often used to accomplish this. The purpose of rough-cut capacity planning is to evaluate the plan prior to attempting to implement it. Sometimes called resource requirements planning.

ROUTING   A document detailing the manufacture of a particular item. It includes the operations to be performed, their sequence, the various work centers to be involved, and the standards for set-up and run. In some companies, the routing also includes information on tooling, operator skill levels, inspection operations, testing requirements, etc.

SAFETY STOCK   In general, a quantity of stock planned to be available to protect against fluctuations in demand and/or supply.

SAFETY TIME   A technique in MRP whereby material is planned to arrive ahead of the requirement date. The difference between the requirement date and the planned in-stock-date is safety time.

SCHEDULED RECEIPTS   Within MRP, open production orders and open purchase orders are considered as "scheduled receipts" on their due date and will be treated as part of available inventory during the netting process for the time period in question. Scheduled receipt dates and/or quantities are not normally altered automatically by the computer. Further, scheduled receipts are not exploded into requirements for components, as MRP logic assumes that all components required for the manufacture of the item in question have either been allocated or issued to the shop floor.

SCRAP FACTOR   A percentage factor used by MRP to increase gross requirements of a given component to account for anticipated loss of that component during the manufacture of its parent.

SERVICE PARTS   Parts used for the repair and/or maintenance of a product. Also called repair parts, spares.

SHOP FLOOR CONTROL   A system for utilizing data from the shop floor as well as data processing files to maintain and communicate status information on shop orders (manufacturing orders) and work centers. The major subfunctions of shop floor control are: 1) assigning priority of each shop order, 2) maintaining work-in-process quantity information, 3) conveying shop order status information, 4) providing actual input and output data for capacity control purposes, 5) providing quantity by location by shop order for work-in-process inventory and accounting purposes, 6) providing measurement of efficiency, utilization and productivity of manpower and machines.

SHOP ORDER CLOSE-OUT STATION   A stocking point on the shop floor. Completed production of components is transacted (received) into the shop order close-out station and subsequently transacted (issued) to assembly or other "downstream" operations. This technique is used to reduce material handling by not having to move items into and out of stockrooms, while simultaneously enabling a high degree of inventory record accuracy.

SHRINKAGE FACTOR   A factor used in material requirements planning which compensates for expected loss during the manufacturing cycle either by increasing the gross requirements or by reducing the expected completion quantity of planned and open orders. The shrinkage factor differs from the scrap factor in that the former affects all uses of the part and its components. The scrap relates to only one usage.

SIMULATION   Within MRP II, utilizing the operational date to perform "what-if" evaluations of alternative plans, to answer the question "Can we do it?" If yes, the simulation can then be run in financial mode to help answer the question "Do we really want to?"

TIME BUCKET   A number of days of data summarized into one columnar display. A weekly time bucket in MRP would contain all the relevant planning data for an entire week. Weekly time buckets are considered to be the largest possible (at least in the near- and medium-term) to permit effective MRP.

TIME FENCE   Point in time where various restrictions or changes in operating procedures take place. For example, changes to the master production schedule can be accomplished easily beyond the cumulative lead time; whereas, changes inside the cumulative lead time become increasingly more difficult, to a point where changes should be resisted. Time fences can be used to define these points.

TWO-LEVEL MPS   A master scheduling approach for make-to-order products where an end product type is master scheduled along with selected key options, features, attachments and common parts.

TURNOVER   The number of times inventory is replaced during a time period; in other words, a measurement of investment inventory to support a given level of sales. It is found by dividing the cost of goods sold for the period by the average inventory for the period.

VENDOR SCHEDULER   A person whose main job is working with vendors regarding what's needed and when. Vendor schedulers are in direct contact with both MRP and the vendors. They do the material planning for the items under their control, communicate the resultant schedules to their assigned vendors, do follow-up, resolve problems, etc. The vendor schedulers are normally organized by commodity, as are the buyers. By using the vendor scheduler approach, the buyers are freed from day-to-day order placement and expediting, and therefore have the time to do cost reduction, negotiation, vendor selection, alternate sourcing, etc. Another term for vendor scheduler is planner/buyer.

VENDOR SCHEDULING   A purchasing approach which provides vendors with schedules rather than individual hard-copy purchase orders. Normally a vendor scheduling system will include a business agreement (contract) for each vendor, a weekly schedule for each vendor extending for some time into the future, and individuals called vendor schedulers. Also required is a formal priority planning system that works very well, because it is essential in this arrangement to provide the vendor with valid due dates routinely.

WORK-IN-PROCESS   Product in various stages of completion

throughout the plant, including raw material that has been released for initial processing and completely processed material awaiting final inspection and acceptance as finished product or shipment to a customer. Many accounting systems also include semi-finished stock and components in this category.

ZERO INVENTORIES   A term adopted by APICS (American Production & Inventory Control Society), the meaning of which is similar to Just-In-Time.

Index